a nordic feast

MIKKEL KARSTAD   PHOTOGRAPHY ANDERS SCHØNNEMANN

a nordic feast

— simple recipes
for gatherings with
friends and family

PRESTEL

MUNICH · LONDON · NEW YORK

preface

My wife and I love gathering a crowd of friends or relations around the table for great conversation while we enjoy fabulous food and have a lovely time together. The joy of socializing is something we want to pass on to our children, and we grab every opportunity to spend quality time with our family.

In this book, I present lots of my favorite recipes for hosting a delicious meal with guests, plus six suggested menus for various events and festive occasions throughout the year: a summer barbecue with fresh seasonal produce, a lavish Sunday brunch to follow an evening of wild partying, a sociable light lunch with extended family, a relaxed mid-week supper with close friends, a festive Christmas dinner packed with family tradition, and a lively and colorful birthday picnic in the garden.

Since every menu is designed for a different occasion, each has its own atmosphere, its own vibe, and its own culinary focus. Many of the dishes have a Scandinavian inspiration; others have Mediterranean, Middle Eastern, or Asian influences. They all reflect the culinary experiences I've collected over the course of my life, which have shaped my style of cooking. Now, I want to share these with other people who are just as passionate as I am about cooking, hosting, and (most importantly of all) enjoying good food together.

Spending time in the physical presence of other people is vital, whether it's friends or family. These moments are so precious, you might even say they are the spice of life. Sadly, many people feel so constrained by their everyday lives, they barely find time to cook, let alone invite guests round. But with a bit of thought, it is eminently possible to fit these kinds of social events into our hectic lives. That is why every menu in this book comes with detailed notes about how and when each dish should be prepared—for example, a couple of days in advance or in the morning before your guests arrive. So, once the guests rock up, you are pretty much free to relax and enjoy the food together, even if you are hosting.

And the menu for a communal meal doesn't always have to be so-phisticated or fancy. The main thing is seeing each other and spending quality time together. You can even organize an event where everyone contributes something to eat. Or you can cook together. There are so many options.

I also encourage you to experiment with the menus and put together recipes that particularly appeal to you. Feel free to leave out the odd dish and add something else instead. Vary the quantities depending on the size of your feast and how many people are coming. I certainly hope my recipes will inspire you to invite people over for food more often, so you can spend more time with the people who enrich your life.

enjoy!
— mikkel karstad

summer barbecue

Campfires, kindling, smoke, and barbecued food. Words that get my culinary pulse racing. This style of cooking and eating is definitely something I want to pass on to my own children.

When you cook over a pure wood fire, you can achieve very high temperatures, giving the grilled food an absolutely exceptional barbecued, smoky flavor. Fish, shellfish, and vegetables are particularly great when prepared this way. They cook in no time at all and are packed with fresh flavor.

It's essential to chop the wood as small as possible, so you can constantly feed the fire with new logs and keep the temperature stable. If the firewood is too big, there will be greater temperature fluctuations, making it harder to control the cooking process. The wood itself should only be glowing because the flames are too hot and will just burn the food on the outside.

Here's my suggested menu for a relaxing summer evening barbecue with fresh, seasonal ingredients that you can enjoy with friends or family. Settle down around the warming fire, which has the added bonus of keeping annoying mosquitoes away!

blackberry juice
with gin and tonic

MAKES 8 GLASSES

1½ cups (200 g) blackberries
   (fresh or frozen)
1 cup (200 g) sugar
5 sprigs mint
Zest and juice of 1 organic lemon
1 cup (240 mL) gin
2 cups (480 mL) tonic water
Ice cubes

Put the blackberries, sugar, sprigs of mint, lemon zest, and juice in a saucepan with 1 cup (240 mL) of water and bring to a boil. Continue boiling for 2–3 minutes, then remove from the heat and leave to infuse (uncovered) for 15–20 minutes at room temperature.

Strain the juice through a fine sieve and cool completely in the fridge.

To serve, put a couple of ice cubes in eight glasses. Then, pour 2 tbsp (30 mL) of gin, ¼ cup (60 mL) of tonic, and ⅛ of the blackberry juice into each glass.

Serve immediately when your guests arrive or with the food. This drink is also deliciously refreshing without the gin.

PREP TIP
You can also make the juice a couple of days in advance and keep it in the fridge until ready to use, ideally in a sealed, sterilized bottle.

fried shrimp
with black currant salt

4¼ cups (1 L) grapeseed oil

4 cups (400 g) fresh medium shrimp,
  shells on

¼ cup (50 g) chickpea (gram) flour

1 tbsp (10 g) freeze-dried black currants

2 tsp (2 g) sea salt

Slowly heat the grapeseed oil in a pan to a temperature of 320°F (160°C).

Toss the shrimp in their shells in the chickpea flour, just enough to give them a light coating, then shake off any excess flour.

Fry the shrimp in batches to make sure the temperature of the oil does not drop too much; cook each batch for about 1 minute, until they are golden and crisp on the outside, tender and juicy on the inside. Scoop the shrimp out of the oil using a slotted spoon, and let them drain on a few layers of paper towels. Fry all the shrimp in the same way. If necessary, allow the oil to return to the required temperature between batches.

Grind the black currants and salt in a pestle and mortar or spice mill until you have a fine red powder.

Sprinkle the fried shrimps with the black currant salt, and serve immediately as a warm snack before the main barbecue.

toasted sourdough bread with chanterelles and corn

SERVES 4

3¾ cups (200 g) fresh chanterelle
    mushrooms
8 thin slices light sourdough bread,
    one day old
4 tbsp (60 mL) olive oil
Sea salt
1 fresh ear of corn
Freshly ground black pepper
Zest and juice of ½ organic lemon

Preheat the oven to 320°F (160°C).

Carefully remove the dirt from the chanterelles using a brush or knife. If any are particularly dirty, you can rinse them briefly under the tap, then dab dry.

Arrange the sourdough bread slices on a baking sheet. Drizzle with 2 tbsp of olive oil and sprinkle lightly with sea salt. Toast the bread in the oven for 7–8 minutes, until crisp and golden brown. Remove from the oven and leave to cool slightly.

Meanwhile, remove the outer leaves and threads from the ear of corn. Cut the kernels of corn from the cob and put them in a bowl.

Heat a pan to a high temperature, add the remaining 2 tbsp of olive oil, and fry the chanterelles for 2–3 minutes, until they are softening and slightly browned. Add the corn and continue frying for 30 seconds. Season with salt and pepper.

Transfer the chanterelles and corn to a bowl and toss in the lemon zest and juice.

Arrange the crisp slices of bread on a platter and top with chanterelles and corn. Serve immediately, while the bread is still crisp and the mushrooms are warm.

PREP TIP
You can toast the bread the previous day and keep it in an airtight container. You can even cook the chanterelles and corn a day ahead of time; in which case, just reheat them briefly before your guests arrive.

bbq skewers with marinated pork neck and rosehip chutney

SERVES 4

Requires: 12 wooden skewers

Timing: Allow 2 hours to soak the wooden skewers and marinate the meat.

ROSEHIP CHUTNEY

3 cups (400 g) fresh rosehips

1 fennel bulb

¼ cup (50 g) sugar

2 star anise pods

5 bay leaves

Sea salt

¾ cup (200 mL) cider vinegar

MARINATED PORK NECK

2 tbsp soy sauce

2 tbsp cider vinegar

2 tbsp red Thai chili paste

1 tbsp acacia honey

2 tbsp olive oil

Salt

Freshly ground black pepper

14 oz (400 g) free-range pork neck

For the chutney, wash the rosehips and slice them in half lengthwise. Scrape out the seeds and all the little hairs with a spoon. Wear gloves to do this, if possible, as the inside of the rosehips can cause itching (in fact, the hairs are used in itching powder). Finely chop the rosehips and put them in a bowl.

Trim the base and tops of the fennel bulbs, then cut them in half lengthwise and slice very thinly. Transfer the sliced fennel to a bowl of cold water to remove any residual sand or dirt.

Gently heat the sugar in a pan until it has dissolved and caramelized to a pale brown color. Add the star anise, bay leaves, sea salt, and fennel. Caramelize everything for 1–2 minutes, until the fennel begins to exude some liquid.

Add the rosehips and continue cooking for 1–2 minutes. Then, pour in the cider vinegar and simmer over low heat for 20–25 minutes to create a thick chutney. This should have a harmonious blend of sweet and sour notes.

Remove the chutney from the heat, and let it cool to allow the flavors to infuse. If necessary, adjust to taste with additional salt, cider vinegar, and/or sugar. Set aside.

For the marinated pork neck, soak the wooden skewers in water for 2 hours to ensure that they do not burn on the barbecue.

Whisk together the soy sauce, cider vinegar, chili paste, honey, olive oil, and salt and pepper to taste in a bowl to create a thick marinade.

Chop the pork neck into cubes (roughly ½ in/1 cm thick) and toss well in the marinade. Marinate for 1–2 hours in the fridge.

Preheat an outdoor grill to high heat.

Slide the cubes of meat onto the skewers and refrigerate until ready to use. As soon as the barbecue is ready, place the skewers on the very hot grill. Cook the meat for 1–2 minutes on each side, so it acquires a lovely grill pattern but remains tender and juicy inside.

Remove the skewers from the grill and drizzle with some of the chutney. Serve immediately with the remaining chutney in a bowl alongside.

PREP TIP

The rosehip chutney is best prepared the previous day and refrigerated to allow the flavors to develop. Ideally, soak the skewers and marinate the meat a day in advance, too. The prepared skewers can then be kept in the fridge until ready to use.

tomato tart with cream cheese, salted onions, and herbs

2 onions

Sea salt

9½ oz (270 g) store-bought puff pastry,
    thawed overnight in the fridge if frozen

⅓ cup (100 g) ricotta

2½ cups (500 g) mixed cherry tomatoes

Leaves from 10 sprigs tarragon

Leaves from 6 sprigs marjoram

3½ tbsp (50 mL) olive oil

Freshly ground black pepper

Preheat the oven to 400°F (200°C). Line a large baking sheet with parchment paper.

Peel, halve, and thinly slice the onions, then place them in a large bowl and sprinkle with a pinch of salt. Massage the salt vigorously into the onion slices until they are soft and exuding some liquid.

Spread the puff pastry on a work surface. Put an 11-inch (28-cm) round plate on top as a template, and cut around the edges of the plate with a sharp knife. Transfer the circle of pastry to the prepared baking sheet. Keep the rest of the pastry in the fridge for another recipe (it will keep for up to 2 days in a sealed container).

Spread the ricotta evenly over the pastry, leaving a gap of about ½ inch (1 cm) around the edge. Spread the onions on top of the ricotta.

Cut the tomatoes into halves, quarters, or small chunks, depending on their size. Set some of the whole tarragon and marjoram leaves aside for a garnish. Roughly chop the remaining leaves and mix in a bowl with the tomatoes, the olive oil, and some salt and pepper.

Spread the tomato mixture over the pastry. Bake the tart for 18–20 minutes, until the puff pastry is crisp and golden and the tomatoes are soft.

Remove the tart from the oven, sprinkle with the reserved whole herb leaves (including some marjoram flowers if you have any), and serve immediately, while it is still hot and crisp.

PREP TIP
The tart can also be baked the previous day, then reheated briefly before serving.

grilled zucchini with ricotta, hazelnuts, mint, and tarragon

SERVES 4

2 zucchini (courgettes)
4 tbsp (60 mL) olive oil
Sea salt
5 tbsp (40 g) hazelnuts
3 sprigs mint
3 sprigs tarragon
⅓ cup (100 g) ricotta
Zest and juice of 1 organic lemon
Freshly ground black pepper

Preheat an outdoor grill to high heat.

Slice the zucchini in half lengthwise; and drizzle the cut sides with half of the olive oil, and sprinkle with salt.

Grill the zucchini halves for about 2 minutes on each side, until they are browning nicely but still retain a bit of bite in the middle. Remove the zucchini from the grill and transfer to a serving dish.

Roughly chop the hazelnuts. Strip the leaves from the mint and tarragon sprigs; discard the stems.

Crumble the ricotta over the grilled zucchini, then drizzle with the lemon juice. Garnish with lemon zest, hazelnuts, and mint and tarragon leaves. Season to taste with salt and pepper, then drizzle with the remaining olive oil.

Serve the grilled zucchini with the rest of your barbecue menu.

yellow split pea purée with marjoram and grilled radishes

1½ cups (300 g) yellow split peas

1 tbsp dried chamomile flowers

⅔ cup (150 mL) olive oil, plus more
    for the radishes

3½ tbsp (50 mL) cider vinegar

Sea salt

Freshly ground black pepper

16 French breakfast radishes

Leaves from ¼ bunch fresh marjoram

Wash the split peas under cold, running water, then cover with fresh water in a saucepan. Add the chamomile flowers and bring to a boil. Lower the temperature and simmer the split peas for about 45 minutes (follow the instructions on the pack), until they are soft and beginning to disintegrate. You may need to drain any remaining water; if you do, save it in case you need to dilute the purée later.

Use a food processor to purée the hot split peas with the olive oil, vinegar, and salt and pepper to taste. If necessary, add some of the reserved split pea cooking water for a runnier consistency. Let the purée cool slightly, then season with more salt, pepper, and vinegar as desired.

Preheat an outdoor grill to high heat.

Wash the radishes, and remove the roots and any wilting leaves. Toss the radishes in olive oil with the green leaves still attached, then grill them on both sides until they have some color but still retain their bite. Only cook the radish greens very briefly, then make sure they hang down over the side of the grill.

Spread the split pea purée across a serving platter and arrange the grilled radishes on top. Then, scatter the radishes with fresh marjoram and serve with the rest of your barbecued food.

PREP TIP

You can make the split pea purée the previous day. Just keep it in the fridge until required.

grilled lettuce hearts with kimchi dressing, seaweed, and sesame seeds

SERVES 4

4 hearts romaine lettuce

⅓ cup (50 g) kimchi (homemade, p. 70, or store-bought)

3½ tbsp (50 mL) olive oil

Sea salt

Freshly ground black pepper

1 tbsp crumbled dried seaweed (feel free to use a mix of several varieties)

1 tbsp sesame seeds

Preheat an outdoor grill to high heat.

Cut the lettuce hearts into quarters, rinse them under cold water, and drain well.

Purée the kimchi and olive oil in a food processor to make a creamy dressing.

Place the lettuce hearts on the hot grill and cook for 1–2 minutes, until they are browning nicely, collapsing slightly, but still retaining their structure. Make sure they are grilled, rather than simply steamed. Remove the romaine from the grill and sprinkle with salt and pepper.

Arrange the grilled lettuce hearts on a serving dish and drizzle with the kimchi dressing. Sprinkle the salad with the crumbled seaweed and sesame seeds.

Serve warm with your barbecued food.

trifle with plums, amaretti, and whipped cream

SERVES 4

12 fully ripe plums
2 tbsp runny honey
1 organic lemon
1 tbsp dried rose petals
¾ cup (200 mL) heavy whipping cream
⅓ cup (100 g) full-fat Greek yogurt
1 tsp vanilla sugar
12 store-bought amaretti
   (or 24 amarettini) cookies

Preheat the oven to 250°F (120°C).

Halve the plums, remove the pits, and place the fruit in a baking dish with the cut sides facing up. Drizzle with honey. Quarter the lemon, then squeeze the juice over the plums. Add the squeezed lemon quarters to the dish. Crumble the rose petals and scatter them over the fruit, then mix everything well.

Bake the plums for 15 minutes or until they are soft and have absorbed the honey, lemon, and rose flavors. Remove from the oven and leave to cool completely.

Meanwhile, use an electric mixer to whip the heavy cream until it is very thick. In a separate bowl, stir the vanilla sugar into the yogurt until smooth, then fold this mixture into the whipped cream. The result should be a soft and creamy vanilla-scented topping.

Gently crumble the amaretti cookies.

To assemble the trifle: Arrange alternate layers of plums, crumbled amaretti, and cream in decorative glasses until all the ingredients have been used.

This trifle is an impressive way to round off a wonderful summer barbecue.

PREP TIP
The plums can be baked the day before and kept in the fridge. You can also assemble the trifle a few hours in advance, so you can give your guests your full attention in the evening. Choose a high-quality product when buying the amaretti cookies—they're worth it!

summer barbecue
— menu planning
and preparation

On a mild summer's evening, it is hard to beat a barbecue in the garden with wonderful company. If you want this to be a relaxing affair—with plenty of time to spend with your guests, even if you are hosting—you should choose simple recipes. Planning is important here. If most dishes are ready ahead of time, you can devote all your attention to your guests and get maximum enjoyment from the evening.

THE PREVIOUS DAY

BLACKBERRY JUICE WITH GIN AND TONIC (P. 16)
Prepare the juice the previous day (or even a couple of days in advance), and leave it to infuse in the fridge until required.

**TOASTED SOURDOUGH BREAD WITH
CHANTERELLES AND CORN (P. 20)**
Toast the bread the previous day, and store it in an airtight container until ready to use.

**BBQ SKEWERS WITH MARINATED PORK NECK
AND ROSEHIP CHUTNEY (P. 23)**
Make the rosehip chutney the previous day, and allow the flavors to infuse in the fridge until required.

**YELLOW SPLIT PEA PURÉE WITH MARJORAM
AND GRILLED RADISHES (P. 30)**
Make the split pea purée the previous day, and store it in the fridge.

**TRIFLE WITH PLUMS, AMARETTI,
AND WHIPPED CREAM (P. 36)**
Bake the plums the previous day; their flavors will be enhanced after their time in the fridge.

BARBECUE

Get the grill ready in the morning by making sure you have charcoal/wood and paper/lighters. Before your guests arrive, all you have to do is strike a match, and your barbecue will soon be at the required temperature. If you are using a propane grill, preheat the grill just before your guests arrive.

TOASTED SOURDOUGH BREAD WITH
CHANTERELLES AND CORN (P. 20)

Prepare the chanterelles and corn in the morning, store them in the fridge, and reheat briefly before serving.

BBQ SKEWERS WITH MARINATED PORK NECK
AND ROSEHIP CHUTNEY (P. 23)

In the morning, soak the wooden skewers in water and marinate the meat. After 1–2 hours, slide the cubes of meat onto the skewers, then store them in the fridge until you're ready to cook.

TOMATO TART WITH CREAM CHEESE,
SALTED ONIONS, AND HERBS (P. 26)

Bake the tart in the morning, then reheat it in the evening to serve.

TRIFLE WITH PLUMS, AMARETTI,
AND WHIPPED CREAM (P. 36)

Assemble the trifle a couple of hours before your guests arrive, and refrigerate it until you're ready to serve.

FINAL ARRANGEMENTS

The final preparations should all be complete before your guests are due, so once they arrive there isn't much more to accomplish—except grill the food. And that is a nice, relaxed activity that can be done while socializing with a drink in one hand.

CLEARING UP

Dirty dishes can easily be left for the following morning, so nothing can distract you from the evening itself. If a couple of the guests live nearby, they may be happy to pop round and help (while enjoying a drink).

sunday brunch

Our everyday lives are incredibly hectic, so my wife Camilla and I always enjoy the time we have together early on weekend mornings. For us, the day starts with a dip in the sea, followed by breakfast. For many years, our favorite options included homemade sourdough rolls, pancakes, yogurt with granola, and fruit juice. But these days, after several trips to Asia, other dishes are increasingly part of our morning routine.

This culinary variety is something our kids have also come to appreciate. They often invite friends over for brunch and have discovered the therapeutic benefits of food that is savory, spicy, and high in fat when recovering from a wild night of partying.

All the brunch preparations are done the previous day. That way, our kids and their friends can rave to their heart's content in the evening and meet up the next morning to cook, eat, play games, and have fun together. I love the fact that they have instigated this tradition, so the following brunch menu is dedicated to them.

To start with, there are a couple of snacks to keep people going while everyone gets on with preparing the rest of the food. All the dishes are then served on a big dining table, so everyone can eat together while sipping tea and catching up on news from the previous evening.

refreshing herbal tea

MAKES 1 LARGE TEAPOT

6¼ cups (1½ L) water
5 sprigs mint
5 sprigs wood sorrel
5 sprigs lemon balm
1 organic lime

Pour the water into a kettle, and bring it to a boil.

Rinse the herbs, and put them in a large teapot.

Slice the lime in half, and squeeze the juice from one half into the teapot. Cut the other half in two, then into slices; add these to the teapot. Pour in the boiling water and leave to infuse for 2–3 minutes.

Serve hot with your Sunday brunch. Fish out the herbs and lime after no more than 15 minutes of steeping.

TIP
A couple of thin slices of organic ginger make a wonderful alternative option in this tea. You can also drink it chilled with a couple of ice cubes.

cold matcha and
almond milk

SERVES 4

1 tbsp matcha powder

3½ tbsp (50 mL) hot water

1¾ cups (420 mL) vegan almond milk

1 tsp ground cinnamon

10 mint leaves

Put the matcha powder in a high-sided bowl, pour in the hot water, and stir.

Add the almond milk, cinnamon, and mint leaves. Use a hand blender to purée everything until you have a smooth, pale green drink.

Pour into a small jug or straight into cups or glasses, and serve as a cold drink with your Sunday brunch.

salad wraps with squid, papaya, lime, and chili pepper

SERVES 4

1 head romaine lettuce

3½ oz (100 g) cleaned and
    prepared baby squid

1 tbsp olive oil

1 lime

Sea salt

½ orange papaya

½ red chili pepper

Remove the core from the head of lettuce and separate the individual leaves. Wash the leaves carefully in a bowl of cold water, then drain well.

Cut the squid into very narrow strips.

Heat the olive oil in a skillet until it is nice and hot. Fry the squid for about 30 seconds, until just cooked but still beautifully soft and tender. If you fry the squid for too long or at too low a temperature, it becomes tough and rubbery.

Meanwhile, squeeze the lime. Remove the squid from the skillet, and transfer it to a dish. Add some sea salt and the lime juice.

Peel the papaya half, scrape out the seeds, and cut it into very thin slices.

Remove the seeds from the chili pepper, then slice it into very thin rings.

Arrange the lettuce leaves on a serving dish or large plate. Add a couple pieces of squid, papaya, and chili pepper to each leaf. Drizzle with lime juice and sprinkle with sea salt.

Serve these wraps as finger food before the other brunch dishes are brought to the table.

crispy noodles
with curry salt

SERVES 4

1 tsp salt
1 tsp curry powder
4¼ cups (1 L) grapeseed oil
7 oz (200 g) gluten-free brown rice noodles

Mix the salt and curry powder in a dish.

Slowly heat the oil in a pan to a temperature of 320–340°F (160–170°C). Immerse the rice noodles in batches in the hot oil and fry for 15–20 seconds, until they "puff up." They will become nice and crisp and turn a golden yellow color. Do not let them get too dark! Scoop the noodles out of the oil with a slotted spoon, and transfer them to a paper towel-lined plate to drain. Continue in the same way until you have fried all the noodles.

Sprinkle the noodles with the curry powder and salt while they are still warm to ensure that they absorb the flavor well.

Serve as a snack before the other brunch dishes are brought to the table.

PREP TIP
The noodles can also be fried a day in advance and stored in an airtight container at room temperature. This keeps them nice and crisp until the next day.

meat gyoza

SERVES 4 TO 6

Requires: Bamboo steamer

½ lb (250 g) ground veal
½ lb (250 g) ground pork
1 tsp sea salt
1 egg
5¼ oz (150 g) panko
   (Japanese breadcrumbs)
1 tbsp dried chili flakes
1 tbsp coriander seeds, crushed
½ tsp freshly ground black pepper
2 tbsp grated fresh ginger
1 red onion
1 bunch scallions (spring onions)
2 tbsp soy sauce
1 tbsp sesame oil
Zest and juice of 1 organic lime
1 (11-oz/300-g) pack 4-inch/10-cm
   round gyoza wrappers
Oil for frying

Combine the ground meat and salt in a bowl. Add the egg, panko, chili flakes, coriander seeds, pepper, and ginger. Mix well until everything holds together.

Peel the red onion. Remove the roots and trim the tops from the scallions. Finely chop the red onion and scallions, and mix them into the ground meat. Next, mix in the soy sauce, sesame oil, lime zest and juice. Chill the mixture for 30 minutes in the fridge.

Scoop small spoonfuls of the mixture and shape into little balls. Moisten the edge of each gyoza wrapper slightly with water, and place the balls in the center of the wrapper. Fold one half of the wrapper over the filling, then fold the top edge of each parcel to create narrow pleats. Press the edges firmly together to make sure none of the filling can escape. Set the filled gyoza base-down on your work surface with the pleated edge pointing up. Continue in this way until you have used up all the filling and made lots of lovely gyoza.

Fry and steam the gyoza according to the instructions on p. 60.

PREP TIP
The filling for the gyoza can also be made the day before. The flavors will develop overnight in the fridge.

vegetarian gyoza

SERVES 4 TO 6

Requires: Bamboo steamer

7 oz (200 g) mixed mushrooms
    (e.g. shiitake, oyster mushrooms,
    button mushrooms)
5¼ oz (150 g) pointed cabbage
3½ oz (100 g) carrots
3 scallions (spring onions)
1 garlic clove
1 red onion
3 tbsp rapeseed oil
1 tbsp grated fresh ginger
1 tsp dried chili flakes
1 tsp sea salt
2 tbsp soy sauce
1 tbsp sesame oil
Zest and juice of 1 organic lime
2 tbsp panko (Japanese breadcrumbs)
1 (11-oz/300-g) pack gyoza wrappers
Oil for frying

Clean or peel the mushrooms and vegetables for the filling, then chop them finely.

Heat the rapeseed oil in a pan to a high temperature. Fry the vegetables, ginger, and chili flakes for 5–7 minutes, stirring regularly, until the vegetables soften slightly and exude some liquid. Add the sea salt, soy sauce, sesame oil, and lime zest and juice, then continue frying for 2–3 minutes.

Remove from the heat and transfer the vegetables to a bowl, pouring away any liquid released during the cooking process. Stir in the panko, cover the bowl, and make sure the mixture is chilled in the fridge before being used to fill the gyoza parcels.

Scoop small spoonfuls of the vegetable mixture and shape into little balls. Moisten the edge of each gyoza wrapper slightly with water, and place the balls in the center of the wrapper. Fold one half of the wrapper over the filling, then fold the top edge of each parcel to create narrow pleats. Press the edges firmly together to make sure none of the filling can escape. Set the filled gyoza base-down on your work surface with the pleated edge pointing up. Continue in this way until you have used up all the filling and made lots of lovely gyoza.

Fry and steam the gyoza according to the instructions on p. 60.

PREP TIP
The filling for the gyoza can also be made the day before. The flavors will develop overnight in the fridge.

preparing the gyoza
in the bamboo steamer

You can cook gyoza in various ways, but I like to use a bamboo steamer because it is so fantastically simple.

Ideally, cook the meat and vegetarian gyoza separately, since they have different cooking times. This approach also helps you remember which parcels have which filling when you are ready to serve them.

Bring some water to a boil in a pan. Line the bamboo steamer with parchment paper, making incisions in the paper with a knife to allow the steam to escape.

Gently heat some oil in a skillet. Fry the base of the gyoza parcels for 2–3 minutes, until golden and slightly crisp. The frying process should give them a slightly roasted flavor.

Arrange a layer of gyoza in the steamer basket, cover with the lid, and place the steamer on the pan of boiling water.

Steam the meat gyoza for 15 minutes. The vegetarian gyoza should be steamed for about 6–7 minutes, until the wrappers are cooked.

Remove the gyoza from the steamer and serve immediately; they taste best when freshly prepared and piping hot. You can start enjoying the first gyoza while the next batch is being cooked in the steamer.

Serve with Sweet and Sour Sauce (p. 62) and Soy and Sesame Dip (p. 62) alongside the other brunch recipes.

sweet and sour sauce

MAKES APPROX. 1 CUP (240 ML)

⅔ cup (150 mL) cider vinegar
⅓ cup (80 g) sugar
½ tsp salt
½ fresh red chili pepper
1 thin slice peeled fresh ginger
1 tbsp cornstarch

Combine the cider vinegar, sugar, and salt with 3½ tbsp (50 mL) water in a saucepan.

Thinly slice the chili and add to the pan with the slice of ginger. Bring to a boil, then remove from the heat and allow the flavors to infuse for 5–10 minutes.

Combine the cornstarch and 3½ tbsp (50 mL) of cold water in a bowl to create a thin paste, then stir this into the mixture in the pan. Return the pan to the heat and bring to a boil, stirring constantly until the sauce has thickened slightly. Simmer gently for 1 minute.

Pour the sauce into a bowl and leave to cool. Serve with the hot Meat Gyoza (p. 56) or Vegetarian Gyoza (p. 59).

PREP TIP
This sauce can be made 1–2 days in advance; the flavors will become more intense over time.

soy and sesame dip

MAKES APPROX. ⅔ CUP (160 ML)

3½ tbsp (50 mL) cider vinegar
7 tbsp (100 mL) soy sauce
1 tbsp honey
2 tbsp toasted sesame oil
1 tbsp sesame seeds

Combine the cider vinegar, soy sauce, and honey in a pan. Bring to a boil, reduce the heat to low, and simmer until the liquid has reduced by a third and thickened slightly.

Remove from the heat, then stir in the sesame oil and sesame seeds to create a smooth sauce.

Pour the sauce into a bowl and leave to cool. Serve with the hot Meat Gyoza (p. 56) or Vegetarian Gyoza (p. 59).

PREP TIP
This dip can be made 1–2 days in advance; the flavors will become more intense over time.

spicy noodle salad
with bok choy, chili pepper,
and soybean paste

SERVES 4

NOODLE SALAD

9 oz (250 g) flat rice noodles

2 heads bok choy

3½ oz (100 g) Chinese broccoli (gai lan)
  or other Asian leafy vegetable

2 scallions (spring onions)

1 handful fresh cilantro (coriander)

2 oz (50 g) pea or bean shoots

DRESSING

1 fresh red chili pepper

1 tsp finely grated fresh ginger

3½ tbsp (50 mL) soy sauce

6½ tbsp (60 g) soybean paste (doenjang)
  or white miso paste

1 tsp honey

1 tbsp fish sauce

Juice of 1 lime

Cook the rice noodles according to the package instructions. Drain the noodles in a sieve, and rinse under cold running water to prevent them cooking further and becoming too soft. Tip the noodles into a bowl.

Trim the bok choy, Chinese broccoli, and scallions, and slice them into thin strips. Wash in a bowl of cold water, then drain well. Add the vegetables to the rice noodles and toss until well combined.

To make the dressing, chop the chili pepper very finely, then combine it with the rest of the dressing ingredients and season to taste. Leave the flavors to infuse for 5–10 minutes, then pour the dressing over the noodle salad.

Roughly chop the cilantro. Sprinkle the noodle salad with the shoots and cilantro, toss well, and serve immediately with the rest of your brunch to ensure the vegetables and herbs are crisp and fresh.

PREP TIP

You can prepare the noodles, vegetables, and dressing the day before, then combine everything 5 minutes before serving.

jasmine rice with pickled egg yolks, scallions, and kimchi

SERVES 4

Timing: Start making the pickled egg yolks the day before. If making homemade kimchi, allow 5–7 days for the fermentation process.

PICKLED EGG YOLKS
4 eggs
¾ cup (200 mL) tamari or soy sauce

RICE
1 cup (200 g) jasmine rice
1 tsp salt

4–8 tbsp kimchi (homemade,
    p. 70, or store-bought)
2 scallions (spring onions)

To pickle the egg yolks, separate the eggs, carefully slipping the egg yolks into a bowl, and cover the yolks with the tamari or soy sauce. The egg whites can be frozen or used in another recipe. Cover the bowl of egg yolks, and let them marinate in the fridge for at least 12 hours or until they have developed a slightly chewy texture.

To cook the rice, cover the jasmine rice with cold water in a pan, and wash it by moving your hands in a circular motion through the rice. Drain the water and repeat this process until the water remains clear.

Cover the rice with fresh water, add the salt, and bring to a boil. Put a lid on the pan and reduce the heat to low, then simmer for 20 minutes, remove the pan from the heat, and leave to stand for 5–10 minutes.

To serve: While the rice cooks, remove the roots and tops from the scallions, rinse under cold water, and slice into thin rings.

Top each portion of warm rice with a pickled egg yolk, 1–2 tbsp kimchi, and sliced scallions; serve with the other brunch dishes.

Each person can then stir their own portion to combine the egg yolk with the rice and kimchi immediately before eating.

TIP
If using store-bought kimchi, choose a good-quality organic product.

homemade kimchi

Timing: Allow 5–7 days for fermentation.

2 oz (50 g) garlic cloves

2 oz (50 g) fresh ginger

1 oz (30 g) hot chili powder

7 tbsp (100 mL) apple juice

4 tsp (20 mL) fish sauce

10½ oz (300 g) kohlrabi

7 oz (200 g) carrots

17½ oz (500 g) green cabbage

2 oz (50 g) scallions (spring onions)

14 oz (400 g) napa cabbage

3 tbsp (40 g) coarse sea salt

Peel and finely grate the garlic and ginger. Combine the garlic, ginger, chili powder, apple juice, and fish sauce in a bowl to make the kimchi paste.

Peel the kohlrabi and carrots. Peel off one whole green cabbage leaf, rinse it, and set it aside. Core the remaining cabbage, then cut it into thin wedges. Thinly slice the kohlrabi, carrots, and green cabbage; transfer to a large bowl.

Trim the base of the scallions and napa cabbage; also remove some of the green tops from the scallions. Finely slice the scallions and napa cabbage and mix with the other vegetables. Use your hands to vigorously rub the sea salt and kimchi paste into the vegetables for 5–10 minutes, until everything is slightly soft and exuding some liquid (ideally, use disposable gloves).

Transfer this vegetable mixture, including any liquid, to a sterilized preserving jar. Press everything down firmly with your hands, then cover everything with the reserved green cabbage leaf. The kimchi must be completely covered with liquid. If the kimchi has been massaged properly, this should be sufficient to produce enough liquid. Otherwise, add a bit of water and sea salt if needed.

There must be a gap of 1–1½ inches (3–4 cm) between the kimchi and the lid. Screw on the lid and put the jar on a plate in a dark location. Leave the kimchi to ferment for 5–7 days, ideally at a temperature of 64–68°F (18–20°C). The fermentation process may take more or less time, depending on the ambient temperature. Open the jar every day to release the pressure that builds up as the vegetables ferment. Once fermentation is well underway and lots of little bubbles are forming, the kimchi should be transferred to the fridge; otherwise, the lactic acid bacteria will multiply too quickly, making the kimchi too acidic. It's a good idea to test the kimchi after a few days.

TIP
Store the kimchi in the fridge after fermentation. It should keep forever (but must always be covered in brine).

mushroom broth with seaweed and tofu

Timing: Allow 1–2 hours to soak the seaweed.

½ oz (15 g) dried red or brown seaweed
   (e.g. dulse or winged kelp)
3¼ cups (800 mL) vegetable broth
2 oz (50 g) dried mushrooms
   (e.g. shiitake or black trumpet)
1–2 tbsp tamari
3 oz (80 g) natural tofu
2 fresh king oyster mushrooms
1 scallion (spring onion)

Soak the seaweed in a bowl of cold water for 1–2 hours, then drain.

Combine the broth, dried mushrooms, and soaked seaweed in a pan. Bring to a boil, reduce the heat to low, and simmer for 1–2 minutes. Remove the pan from the heat and leave to stand for 15–20 minutes to allow the seaweed and mushrooms to infuse the broth with flavor.

Pour the bouillon through a sieve into a second saucepan (set aside the mushrooms and seaweed). Reheat the broth and season to taste with tamari.

Chop the mushrooms and seaweed into bite-size pieces; add to the broth.

Dice the tofu into ½-inch (1-cm) cubes. Thinly slice the king oyster mushrooms. Stir both into the broth and heat briefly.

Trim the roots and tops from the scallion, then slice thinly. Divide the broth among soup dishes, including some mushrooms, seaweed, and tofu in each dish, then scatter with sliced scallion and serve with the rest of your brunch menu.

PREP TIP
This broth can be prepared the previous day; in which case, just add the tofu and other ingredients shortly before serving. When your guests arrive, heat it up and garnish with scallions.

mango with fermented honey, lime, and black sesame seeds

SERVES 4

Timing: Allow 3–4 days to ferment the honey.

Honey

2 very ripe mangos

Zest and juice of 2 limes

2 tbsp black sesame seeds

It is worth making a bigger batch of fermented honey than required for this recipe. Take as much honey as you want, and mix it with water as described below using a ratio of 10:1 (e.g., 3½ oz/100 g honey with 0.35 fl oz/10 mL water).

Mix the honey and water until well combined. Allow to ferment at room temperature in an open jar for 3–4 days. It will be a bit bubbly inside and frothy on top.

Peel the mangos, cut the fruit away from the stones, and slice it into thin wedges.

Arrange the mango slices on a serving dish or individual plates. Drizzle with 2 tbsp fermented honey and the lime juice, then sprinkle with the lime zest and black sesame seeds.

Serve as a refreshing dessert at the end of your Sunday brunch.

TIP

Store the remaining honey at room temperature in an open or loosely covered jar (not in the fridge, as this will make it set too hard). It will become even more aromatic over time, and depending on the type of honey you use, it will take on sweet and tangy or even yeasty flavors, which can enhance a variety of different dishes and drinks.

sunday brunch
— menu planning and preparation

Inviting friends for a weekend brunch is always a pleasure—even if you are out late the night before. It doesn't take long to plan and prepare a good brunch, and, particularly after a wild party, it is great to hang out with friends to chat about the previous evening and combat your hangover with some salty, spicy, and/or fatty food.

THE PREVIOUS WEEK

KIMCHI (P. 70)
Make the kimchi 5–7 days before your brunch to ensure a rich flavor.

FERMENTED HONEY (P. 76)
Start fermenting the honey at room temperature 3–4 days beforehand.

1–2 DAYS IN ADVANCE

SHOPPING
Get the shopping done early (ideally on Friday or Saturday) to make sure you have time to source unusual ingredients and have everything ready for the day itself.

SWEET AND SOUR SAUCE + SOY AND SESAME DIP (P. 62)
Make the sauce and dip 1–2 days in advance; the earlier you make them, the more delicious they will be.

THE PREVIOUS DAY

CRISPY NOODLES WITH CURRY SALT (P. 55)
Fry the noodles the previous day, and store them in an airtight container to keep them nice and crisp. The added bonus in this approach is that the smell of fried fat will have disappeared from your kitchen by the time your guests arrive.

MEAT GYOZA (P. 56)
VEGETARIAN GYOZA (P. 59)
Make the fillings for the gyoza the previous day, and store them overnight in the fridge.

SPICY NOODLE SALAD WITH BOK CHOY, CHILI PEPPER, AND SOYBEAN PASTE (P. 66)

You can cook the noodles and vegetables and make the dressing for the salad the previous day. Just mix everything together 5 minutes before serving.

PICKLED EGG YOLKS (P. 69)

Get the egg yolks ready the previous evening, and marinate them in the fridge overnight (for at least 12 hours).

MUSHROOM BROTH WITH SEAWEED AND TOFU (P. 73)

Cook the broth the previous day, and store it in the fridge overnight. When you're ready to serve the broth, heat it in a pan with the other ingredients.

ON THE DAY ITSELF

To make sure your Sunday gets off to a relaxed start, you can finish off the last few details in the company of your guests. It's more fun doing things this way! Everyone can choose a task that appeals to them: One person might finish cooking a particular dish, someone else can set the table, and others can simply chat, chill out, and provide the special vibe that goes with a leisurely Sunday brunch.

family lunch

I love the Italian tradition of gathering the entire family at the week-end—including kids, parents, and grandparents—to cook together, then enjoy a long, leisurely lunch. We have tried to introduce this tradition in our own family by enjoying a midday or evening meal together every Sunday.

Italian cuisine and lifestyle are a huge source of inspiration for me, both as a professional chef and when cooking at home for my family. In Italy, there is a great emphasis on allowing the ingredients to speak for themselves, each revealing its own specific flavor. I love this approach, and it's something I try to achieve in my own kitchen.

The most important thing about this lunch or supper is spending time together, something that is sadly often in short supply during the week. Needless to say, enjoying delicious food is also an essential component.

At our Sunday get-togethers, we always stick to simple dishes that are easy to combine and complement each other beautifully—all served with some good bread. So, the following suggested menu consists of straightforward recipes, many of which can be made in advance to avoid too much work on the day itself. The focus should be on enjoying each other's company rather than elaborate cooking.

rhubarb juice with lemon, mint, and geranium

MAKES APPROX. 12¾ CUPS (3 L)
JUICE

2¼ lbs (1 kg) rhubarb
1½ cups (300 g) sugar
2 organic lemons
Blossoms from 3 sprigs scented geranium
Leaves from 5 sprigs mint

Trim the rhubarb, making sure you don't remove too much of the base of each stalk, as this is particularly rich in juice and energy. Wash the stalks in cold water, then chop them into little pieces.

Transfer the chopped rhubarb to a saucepan, along with the sugar and 8½ cups (2 L) of water. Halve the lemons, add them to the pan, and bring everything to a boil. Lower the temperature and simmer gently for 5 minutes. Remove the pan from the heat and add the geranium blossoms and mint leaves. Cover and allow to infuse for 20–25 minutes.

Strain the juice through a muslin cloth or fine-mesh sieve to ensure you get a nice clear liquid, then pour into sterilized bottles and refrigerate until ready to serve.

This is a wonderfully refreshing beverage to serve with any of the dishes from the lunch menu—and of course it also makes an ideal drink to raise a toast.

PREP TIP
If you make the juice the previous day, its flavor will develop even more overnight. You can even keep it in the fridge for 2–3 weeks.

sprats with tomato chutney

SERVES 4

1 medium onion

1 tbsp sugar

1 star anise pod

5 fennel seeds

1 tsp sea salt

3 large tomatoes

3½ tbsp (50 mL) cider vinegar

3½ tbsp (50 mL) olive oil

1 (3½-oz/100-g) tin Fangst brand sprats
  or tinned sardines

Peel and halve the onion, then slice it very thinly.

Heat the sugar, star anise, and fennel seeds in a pan over medium heat until the sugar is pale brown and caramelized and the spices have begun to release their fragrance. Add the onion and salt, then cook gently until the onion has softened and is beginning to exude some liquid.

Roughly chop the tomatoes, stir these into the onions, and simmer for 2–3 minutes, until they are slightly disintegrating. Stir in the cider vinegar, reduce the heat, and simmer everything down until you have a creamy chutney.

Check the taste and add more salt, sugar, or vinegar to achieve the desired sweet and sour flavor. Finally, carefully stir in the olive oil.

Transfer the tomato chutney to a bowl and leave to cool slightly. It should be served at room temperature.

Either serve the sprats straight from the tin or arrange them on a plate; serve with tomato chutney and toast.

PREP TIP

The tomato chutney can easily be made the previous day (or several days in advance). It will keep for about 1 week in the fridge in a sterilized preserving jar.

pickled vegetables with fennel, chili, and chamomile flowers

MAKES 1 LARGE PRESERVING JAR
(ROUGHLY 67 FL OZ/2 L)

Timing: Start 2–3 days in advance.

2 carrots

1 fennel bulb

2 red bell peppers

1 small head cauliflower

2 tbsp sea salt

4¼ cups (1 L) cider vinegar

2½ cups (500 g) sugar

1 tbsp fennel seeds

1 tbsp dried chamomile flowers

3 star anise pods

1 fresh licorice root

1 red chili pepper

2 garlic cloves

Peel the carrots. Remove the green fronds from the fennel and trim off the base of the bulb. Halve the bell peppers and remove the membranes and seeds. Remove the outer green leaves from the cauliflower.

Chop the carrots, fennel, and bell peppers into ¾-inch (2-cm) pieces. Split the cauliflower into florets.

Sprinkle the vegetables with the salt in a bowl, rubbing it in well. Leave this mixture to stand for 2–3 hours at room temperature. Then, layer everything up in a large (2-L) preserving jar.

Put the cider vinegar, sugar, fennel seeds, chamomile flowers, star anise, licorice, and whole chili pepper in a saucepan with 4¼ cups (1 L) of water. Peel the garlic cloves and add them to the pan. Bring to a boil.

As soon as the liquid boils, pour it over the vegetables in the jar. Seal the jar, let cool, then refrigerate for 2–3 days to allow the flavors to infuse.

Serve the pickles as a refreshing side with the rest of the lunch menu.

PREP TIP
You can make the pickles a few days in advance (or even further ahead). They will keep in a sealed jar in the fridge for 1–2 months, provided that the vegetables are always covered in the preserving liquid.

marinated anchovy fillets

SERVES 4

Timing: Allow 3–4 hours to marinate the anchovies.

14 oz (400 g) fresh anchovies
3 tbsp sea salt

MARINADE
1 garlic clove
1 organic lemon
1 tsp whole pink peppercorns
4 tbsp elderflower vinegar
7 tbsp (100 mL) olive oil

Carefully wash the outsides and inside cavities of the anchovies. Remove the heads, pulling out the backbones at the same time. Leave the tail. You can also ask your trusted fishmonger to carry out this step for you. Carefully rinse the anchovies again in cold water and dab dry with kitchen paper. Put the fish in a bowl, sprinkle with sea salt, then leave at room temperature for 2–3 hours. At the end of this period, dab away any excess salt from the fish.

To make the marinade, finely slice the garlic, then zest the lemon. Combine the garlic, lemon zest, pink peppercorns, elderflower vinegar, and olive oil in a large bowl.

Add the anchovies to the bowl, turning to coat them in the marinade, then cover and refrigerate for 3–4 hours before serving.

Enjoy the anchovies with toasted bread, which you can dip in the delicious marinade.

PREP TIP
You can also make the anchovies the previous day or several days in advance and keep them in the fridge in the marinade.

mussels with zucchini, almonds, chili, and bronze fennel

SERVES 4

½ zucchini (courgette)

¼ red chili pepper

¼ cup (30 g) almonds

Zest and juice of 1 organic lemon

2 tbsp olive oil

Sea salt

Freshly ground black pepper

1 (3½-oz/100-g) tin Fangst brand
    blue mussels preserved in oil with
    dill and fennel seeds

Handful of bronze fennel sprigs,
    with flowers if possible

Wash and finely dice the zucchini, then transfer to a bowl.

Remove the seeds from the chili pepper, then chop with the almonds and combine both ingredients with the diced zucchini. Add the lemon zest and juice, olive oil, and salt and pepper to taste. Mix everything well.

Tip the tinned mussels into a deep dish, including the liquid.

Arrange the zucchini and chili mixture on top of the mussels. Remove the stalks from the sprigs of bronze fennel, and use the fronds to garnish the mussels.

Serve with focaccia (p. 107) or toast for lunch.

white beans with vegetables and parmesan

SERVES 4

Timing: Start the previous day.

7 oz (200 g) dried white beans

1 carrot

1 garlic clove

1 medium onion

2 medium tomatoes

1 sprig rosemary

3½ tbsp (50 mL) olive oil,
   plus more for drizzling

2 tbsp cider vinegar

Sea salt

Freshly ground black pepper

½ cup (50 g) freshly grated parmesan

Soak the beans in plenty of cold water for 24 hours.

The next day, drain the beans, place them in a saucepan, and cover with fresh water.

Peel the carrot, garlic, and onion, chop into small pieces, and add to the pan with the beans. Bring everything to a boil, and scoop off any foam that rises to the surface with a slotted spoon.

Halve the tomatoes and stir them into the beans with the sprig of rosemary. Cook for 30–35 minutes, until the beans are cooked.

Use a slotted spoon to transfer two-thirds of the beans from the pan into a bowl. Mix these beans with 1 tbsp each of olive oil and cider vinegar, season to taste with plenty of sea salt and freshly ground pepper, then set aside.

Continue cooking the rest of the beans for 10–15 minutes, until they are very soft. Remove the pan from the heat and stir the remaining 2½ tbsp of olive oil and cider vinegar into the bean mixture, along with most of the Parmesan.

Remove the sprig of rosemary, then use an immersion blender to purée the beans and vegetables until smooth. Carefully mix in the beans you set aside earlier. Season to taste with salt, pepper, and maybe some more cider vinegar.

Serve the beans lukewarm with a splash of olive oil and the rest of the grated Parmesan.

PREP TIP

You can start soaking the beans 2–3 days in advance; just cook and prepare the beans the next day. Store the bean purée in the fridge, reheat slightly before serving, and check whether it requires any additional seasonings.

whole artichokes with capers, cream cheese, and verbena

SERVES 4

4 large artichokes
1 organic lemon
Sea salt
¾ cup (150 g) cream cheese
2 tbsp capers
1 handful common verbena
   (or mint leaves)
Olive oil
Freshly ground black pepper

Snap the stalks off the artichokes, making sure you remove the hairs at the base of each stalk.

Cut the lemon into four slices. Use a toothpick to attach 1 slice of lemon to the base of each artichoke to prevent them oxidizing (turning brown) while they cook.

Bring a large pan of slightly salted water to a boil. Simmer the artichokes for 10–15 minutes over low heat and with the lid on. Then, remove from the heat and let the vegetables stand in the cooking water for about 5 minutes. The artichokes are done when you can pull off a leaf with only slight resistance.

Spread the cream cheese on a plate, or put it in a bowl. Chop the capers, and remove the verbena leaves from the stems. Garnish the cream cheese with the capers, verbena leaves, olive oil, and salt and pepper to taste.

Lift the artichokes out of the cooking water, drain, and arrange on a serving dish. Serve the artichokes warm with the garnished cream cheese as part of your lunch menu.

TIP
To eat the artichokes, pull off individual leaves, put a bit of cream cheese on the thick end of each leaf, then scrape the flesh of the artichoke off the leaf with your front teeth.

buttermilk focaccia with wild herbs, mozzarella, and dulse

MAKES 1 LOAF

Timing: Start the previous evening.

¾ cup + 1 tbsp (200 mL) buttermilk

¾ ounce (20 g) fresh yeast

4 cups + 2 tbsp (500 g) organic
   all-purpose flour

2½ cups (300 g) organic
   Italian type 00 flour

4¼ tsp (20 g) sea salt

4 tbsp (60 mL) extra-virgin olive oil

4 oz (125 g) fresh mozzarella

1 tbsp dried dulse

1 handful fresh wild herbs
   (e.g. nettle leaves)

Start the previous evening by combining 3 cups (700 mL) of cold water with the buttermilk in a bowl, then adding the yeast and stirring to dissolve. Add both flours and 3¼ tsp (15 g) of the sea salt. Stir everything with a wooden spoon until you have a smooth dough.

Cover the dough with a kitchen towel and leave to prove in the fridge for about 12 hours.

The next day, coat a baking sheet with half of the olive oil. Spread the dough out over the sheet, carefully pressing and stretching it out to the sides.

Tear the mozzarella into little pieces and scatter these over the dough.

Gently crush the dulse and distribute this over the dough, along with the wild herbs and the remaining 1 tsp (5 g) of sea salt. Then, brush the focaccia with the remaining olive oil, applying several layers to the dough.

Leave the focaccia dough to prove on the baking sheet for 30–60 minutes at room temperature. Preheat the oven to 450°F (230°C).

Bake the bread for 15 minutes, then lower the oven temperature to 400°F (200°C) and continue baking for 20 minutes or until the focaccia is golden brown.

Remove from the oven and transfer the bread to a wire rack to cool and develop a crisp crust all over.

Serve with your lunch menu to dunk into all the wonderful sauces and mop up every last morsel on your plate.

radicchio with sunflower seed cream and salted gooseberries

SERVES 4

Timing: Allow at least 2 hours for the gooseberries to infuse.

SALTED GOOSEBERRIES
3½ oz (100 g) fresh or frozen gooseberries
1 tbsp sea salt
3½ tbsp (50 mL) olive oil

SUNFLOWER SEED CREAM
¾ cup (100 g) sunflower seeds
1 tsp salt
3½ tbsp (50 mL) olive oil
2 tbsp cider vinegar

2 heads radicchio or red chicory
Olive oil, for drizzling

Preheat the oven to 212°F (100°C). Wash the fresh gooseberries, top and tail them, then transfer to an ovenproof dish (there is no need to defrost frozen gooseberries). Sprinkle the gooseberries with the sea salt and bake for 10–15 minutes. Remove from the oven as soon as they begin to burst and absorb the salt. They should still retain their shape and have some texture. As soon as you take the gooseberries out of the oven, drizzle them with the olive oil. Leave to stand at room temperature for at least 2 hours before serving.

To make the sunflower seed butter, put the seeds in a saucepan, and pour in just enough water to cover the seeds. Add the salt and bring to a boil. Let the seeds boil for 15 minutes or until softened.

Remove the pan from the heat and leave the seeds to stand in the water for 5 minutes. Stir in the olive oil and vinegar, then use an immersion blender to purée the mixture. The result should have a creamy consistency similar to hummus. The cream will thicken as it cools, so don't make it too thick at this stage and add more water if necessary. Allow the cream to cool slightly in a bowl.

Tear off the individual radicchio or chicory leaves and rinse under cold water. Drain well.

Spread the sunflower seed cream over a large serving dish and arrange the salad leaves in a decorative style on top. Scatter the salted gooseberries over the leaves, then drizzle everything with olive oil.

Serve as a refreshing salad with the other lunch dishes.

PREP TIP
The gooseberries can be prepared a few days in advance. They will keep in a closed jar for about 1 week. In the morning, take the required quantity of berries out of the fridge and let them come to room temperature. The sunflower seed cream can also be made the previous day and stored in the fridge.

apricot cake with mascarpone, lemon, and sweet cicely

MAKES 1 (9-INCH/ 22-CM-DIAMETER) CAKE

1¼ cups (200 g) sugar

¾ cup (180 g) butter

Pinch of salt

3 eggs

2 cups + 1 tbsp (250 g) all-purpose flour

2 tsp baking powder

4 tbsp desiccated coconut

Zest and juice of 1 organic lemon

2 tbsp milk

Oil or butter to grease the tin

TOPPING

7 ounces (200 g) mascarpone

8 apricots

Handful of sweet cicely sprigs
(preferably with flowers)

Preheat the oven to 340°F (170°C) (convection setting).

Cream the sugar, butter, and salt in the bowl of an electric mixer. Add the eggs one at a time, mixing thoroughly before adding the next egg.

Use a wooden spoon or rubber spatula to carefully fold in the flour, baking powder, desiccated coconut, and lemon zest and juice.

Finally, gradually stir in the milk, just until it is fully incorporated. If you overwork the mixture, it may curdle.

Grease a (9-in/22-cm-diameter) springform tin with butter or oil, then pour the cake batter into the tin. Bake the cake for 35–40 minutes. Test whether it is done using a wooden or metal skewer: The cake is ready if the skewer does not have any cake mixture on it after being inserted into the center. Otherwise, bake the cake for a few more minutes, covering the top with aluminum foil if it is browning too much.

Remove the cake from the oven, let it cool slightly on a wire rack, then take it out of the tin to cool completely.

Halve the apricots, remove the stones, and cut the fruit into bite-size pieces. Strip off the sweet cicely leaves and flowers and roughly chop them.

Spread the cooled cake with the mascarpone. Arrange the apricot pieces on top of the cake. Scatter with the chopped sweet cicely leaves and flowers.

This cake is a fabulous way to finish a family lunch.

PREP TIP

The cake tastes best when freshly baked, but it also keeps for a couple of days in an airtight container in the refrigerator.

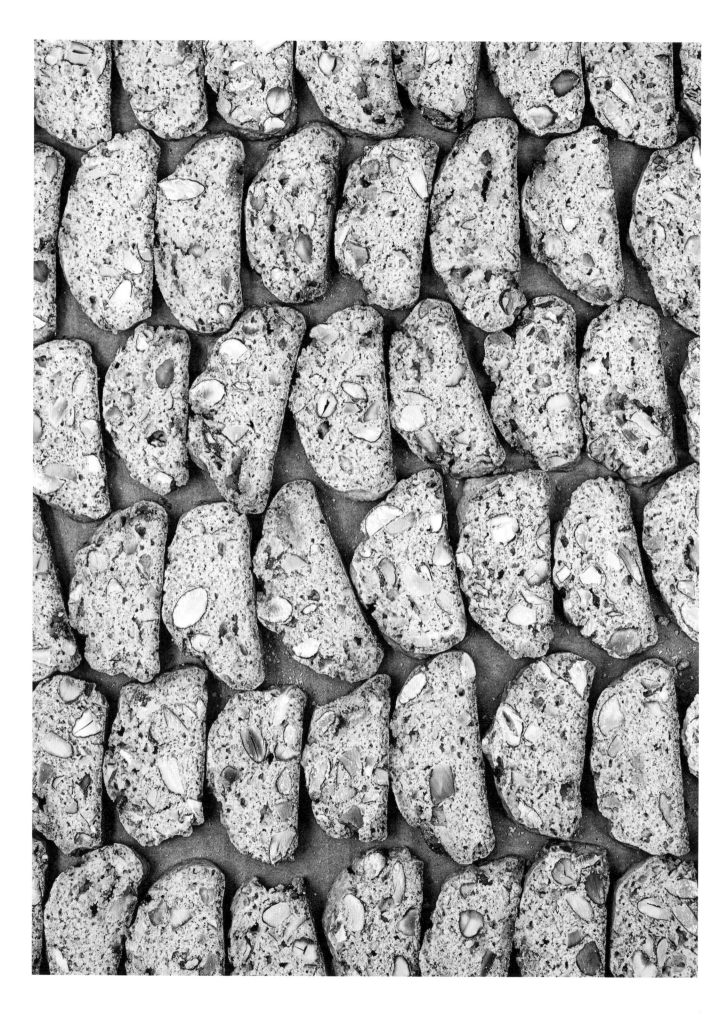

biscotti with nuts, white chocolate, and carrots

MAKES 60–70 BISCOTTI

2½ tbsp (35 g) butter

Pinch of salt

3 eggs

2 egg yolks

1½ cups (300 g) sugar

3½ cups (430 g) all-purpose flour

1 tsp baking powder

9 oz (260 g) mixed nuts (e.g. almonds, pistachios, hazelnuts)

2 oz (50 g) white chocolate

Juice of 1 lemon

½ carrot, grated

Melt the butter with the salt in a pan, then turn off the heat and allow to cool slightly.

Whisk the eggs, egg yolks, and sugar in a bowl until pale and fluffy. Sift the flour and baking powder into a separate bowl, then fold into the egg mixture with a wooden spoon. Chop the nuts and white chocolate and fold these into the mixture, too. Finally, stir in the melted butter with the lemon juice and grated carrot.

Preheat the oven to 300°F (150°C) (convection setting). Line a large baking sheet with parchment paper.

Shape the dough into three narrow logs and transfer to the prepared baking sheet.

Bake the biscotti logs for about 35 minutes, until lightly browned. Remove from the oven and leave to cool briefly on a wire rack. Turn off the oven.

Slice the logs into individual biscotti, then place these back on the baking sheet. Place the baking sheet in the turned-off oven, and let the biscotti dry out in the residual heat for 15–20 minutes.

Serve the biscotti with coffee after your family lunch.

PREP TIP

The biscotti can be baked a few days in advance and stored in an airtight container at room temperature.

family lunch
— menu planning and preparation

It feels like such a gift having the whole family gathered around the table to eat, even if you're not marking any special occasion. Best of all is when you manage to get several generations together. Even for a relaxed lunch of this kind, it really helps to pick straightforward recipes and do as much as you can in advance. Everyone can get involved preparing the ingredients, cooking the food, laying the table, and, in summer, maybe even carrying food out to the garden or terrace.

THE PREVIOUS WEEK

PICKLED VEGETABLES WITH FENNEL, CHILI, AND CHAMOMILE FLOWERS (P. 95)
The vegetables can be pickled the previous week to allow the flavors to develop. Store in the fridge in a sterilized jar, making sure the contents are always covered by the liquid.

BISCOTTI WITH NUTS, WHITE CHOCOLATE, AND CARROTS (P. 117)
Bake the biscotti a few days in advance and store in an airtight container.

THE PREVIOUS DAY

RHUBARB JUICE WITH LEMON, MINT, AND GERANIUM (P. 88)
Make the rhubarb juice the previous day (or several days in advance) and store in the fridge. This drink will taste even better if given time to infuse.

HOMEMADE MARINATED ANCHOVY FILLETS (P. 96)
Prepare the anchovies the previous day (or several days in advance), and keep them in the fridge in the marinade.

SPRATS WITH TOMATO CHUTNEY (P. 92)
Cook the tomato chutney the day before so the flavors can develop while stored in the fridge. This recipe can even be made up to one week ahead of time; in that case, it should be stored in the fridge in a sterilized preserving jar.

BUTTERMILK FOCACCIA WITH WILD HERBS, MOZZARELLA, AND DULSE (P. 107)

Make the focaccia dough the night before and leave to prove in the fridge overnight. The focaccia should be baked the following morning, a couple of hours before your guests arrive.

WHITE BEANS WITH VEGETABLES AND PARMESAN (P. 103)

The beans should be soaked for 24 hours, starting the previous day. Another option is to cook the soaked beans 1–2 days ahead of time, purée them, and store in the fridge. Gently reheat the beans and check the seasoning just before you are ready to serve.

RADICCHIO WITH SUNFLOWER SEED CREAM AND SALTED GOOSEBERRIES (P. 111)

Prepare the gooseberries the previous day, and remove them from the fridge a couple of hours before serving so they come to room temperature. The sunflower seed cream can also be made the previous day and stored in a jar in the fridge.

ON THE DAY ITSELF

In the morning, bake the apricot cake (p. 114) and the focaccia (p. 107). Then, there are just a couple more things to take care of. Shortly before your guests are due, cook the artichokes (p. 104) so they can be eaten fresh, check the seasoning in all the dishes, and make sure everything is ready to serve. Enjoy your meal!

midweek supper

Inviting people over for supper during the week is something many of our friends just never manage. Work, kids, and everyday obligations seem to get in the way. And we all know what it's like trying to get several people together at a weekend. If you're lucky, you might find a suitable date every three or four months. Meeting up during the week, on the other hand, means you can see people more often and enjoy hanging out together.

People often set their expectations too high and feel they have to offer guests several courses of fancy food. I recommend a very different approach. Here's my suggestion for inviting friends over to eat on a completely normal working day. The basic principle is to cook simple, no-nonsense food. Maybe you can even agree that all the guests will make a small contribution to the meal. This makes the host's task much easier.

When we have friends over during the week, we often meet at about 5:30 pm and enjoy a leisurely supper, so we are finished by about 8 and can head our separate ways. After all, everyone needs to be up bright and early the next morning for work. This doesn't prevent us from enjoying a lovely meal together in relaxed company.

hibiscus juice

MAKES 8–10 GLASSES

Timing: Allow 1–2 hours for the juice to infuse.

2 organic lemons
2½ oz (75 g) dried whole hibiscus flowers
1½ cups (250 g) raw cane sugar

Slice the lemons and place them in a saucepan with 6¼ cups (1½ L) of water, the hibiscus flowers, and sugar. Bring everything to a boil, reduce the temperature, and let simmer for 5 minutes. Remove from the heat and let the flavors infuse at room temperature for 1–2 hours. Then, strain the juice through a muslin cloth or fine-mesh sieve.

Serve with plenty of ice cubes for guests to enjoy with their lovely supper menu.

PREP TIP
You can get started making the juice a few days before your supper (or even the previous weekend). This allows the flavors to infuse beautifully.

homemade ginger beer

Timing: Start 2–3 days in advance.

7 oz (200 g) fresh organic ginger

2 organic limes

2 organic lemons

2¼ cups (450 g) sugar

⅓ cup (100 g) honey

3 star anise pods

1 fresh licorice root

10 whole allspice berries

10 whole black peppercorns

Coarsely grate the ginger. Slice the limes and lemons thinly. Place the fruit in a heat-resistant container with a lid, along with the sugar, honey, star anise, licorice, allspice, peppercorns, and ginger.

Bring 10½ cups (2½ L) of water to a boil in a pan and pour it over the fruit-and-spice mixture in the container. Stir everything well, cover, and leave to infuse in the fridge for 2–3 days.

Strain the ginger beer just before serving, add a dash of mineral water and maybe some ice cubes, and offer guests a sparkling drink they can raise as a toast.

PREP TIP

Since the ginger beer needs to infuse, this is best made a few days before your supper (or even the previous weekend).

veggie chickpea tagine with coconut milk and mint

SERVES 4

Timing: Start the previous day.

1 cup (200 g) dried chickpeas
2 red onions
3 garlic cloves
1 red chili pepper
2 tbsp olive oil
2 tsp medium-hot curry powder
2 tsp cumin seeds
3 green cardamom pods
1 tsp coriander seeds
2 tsp garam masala
3 waxy potatoes (e.g. Estima or Marabel)
½ head cauliflower
1 zucchini (courgette)
1¼ cups (300 mL) vegetable broth
1 (14-oz/400-g) can diced tomatoes
1 (13.5-oz/400-mL) can coconut milk
Sea salt
Freshly ground black pepper
1 organic lemon
1 bunch mint

Soak the chickpeas in a bowl with plenty of cold water for 24 hours.

The next day, drain the chickpeas and place them in a saucepan with fresh water. Bring to a boil, lower the heat, and simmer for 30 minutes or until the beans are tender. Drain.

Peel and roughly chop the onions and garlic. Halve the chili pepper, scrape out the seeds, and chop roughly. Heat the olive oil in a large pan. Add the onions, chili, and garlic and sauté for a few minutes, until translucent.

Roughly grind the curry powder, cumin, cardamom, coriander seeds, and garam masala using a food processor or spice grinder. Add to the onion mixture and continue frying for about 1 minute, until the spices release their fragrance.

Peel the potatoes, then chop into rough cubes. Cut the cauliflower and zucchini into cubes about the same size as the potatoes. Add the chopped vegetables to the pan, along with the drained chickpeas, vegetable stock, tomatoes, and coconut milk. Stir to combine. Season to taste with salt and freshly ground black pepper.

Bring the mixture to a boil, reduce the heat, and simmer for 20–25 minutes or until the consistency is creamy and the vegetables are tender. Add some more salt and pepper to the tagine if desired.

Finely zest the lemon and strip the mint leaves from the stalks. Sprinkle the tagine with lemon zest and mint leaves. This makes a wonderful, warming dish to include in your midweek supper menu.

PREP TIP
The tagine can also be made several days in advance; it will develop a more rounded flavor and can be reheated very quickly.

rhubarb m'hamsa with preserved lemons, chili, and parsley

SERVES 4

5 oz (150 g) rhubarb
2 tbsp (25 g) sugar
9 oz (250 g) m'hamsa (hand-rolled
    Tunisian couscous) or pearl couscous
1 tsp sea salt
3½ tbsp (50 mL) olive oil
½ red chili pepper
¼ preserved lemon
1 bunch flat-leaf parsley

Trim the base and leaves from the rhubarb, then rinse the stalks and slice them very thinly. Transfer to a shallow dish. Sprinkle with the sugar and leave at room temperature for 15 minutes.

Place the m'hamsa in a saucepan and pour in enough cool water to cover the couscous by ¾ inch (2 cm). Then, add the sea salt and 2 tbsp of the olive oil.

Bring the m'hamsa to a boil, lower the temperature, and simmer for about 10 minutes or until all the liquid has been absorbed and the couscous is tender. Remove the pan from the heat and let the m'hamsa stand un-covered for 2 minutes.

Scrape the chili pepper to remove the seeds, then chop it very finely with the preserved lemon. Gently stir both ingredients into the m'hamsa, along with the remaining 1½ tbsp of olive oil.

Rinse the parsley in cold water, then chop roughly.

Fold the rhubarb and parsley into the m'hamsa; serve immediately, while the couscous is still warm and the rhubarb is crisp.

PREP TIP
This dish needs a bit of attention just before serving, but the cooked m'hamsa can be combined with the chili and preserved lemon a few hours beforehand; it will just have a stronger flavor. Alternatively, get one of your guests to arrive a bit early so they can make this dish—or they can bring the prepared m'hamsa with them.

veggie galette with herbs and parmesan

SERVES 8–10

2 fennel bulbs

Sea salt

3½ oz (100 g) mascarpone

Freshly ground black pepper

3½ tbsp (50 mL) olive oil

9½ oz (270 g) store-bought puff pastry, thawed overnight in the fridge if frozen

2 zucchini (courgettes)

5 sprigs thyme

5 sprigs rosemary

¼ red chili pepper

Preheat the oven to 400°F (200°C). Line a large baking sheet with parchment paper.

Remove the base and stem ends of the fennel bulbs, then slice them very thinly using a mandoline or sharp knife. Place the sliced fennel in a bowl, sprinkle with 1 tsp of salt, and rub it in until the fennel has softened and is exuding liquid.

In a medium bowl, mix together the mascarpone, a pinch of sea salt, a few grinds of black pepper, and 1 tbsp of the olive oil. Roll out the puff pastry to a 10-inch (25-cm) square, then carefully transfer it to the prepared baking sheet. Spread the mascarpone mixture evenly over the pastry, leaving a ½-inch (1-cm) border around the edge.

Scatter the sliced fennel on top of the mascarpone.

Slice the zucchini lengthwise into quarters, then chop into small pieces. Remove the seeds from the chili pepper, then chop it very finely with the thyme and rosemary. Mix these chopped ingredients with the remaining 2½ tbsp of olive oil, salt, and pepper in a bowl. Toss the zucchini in this mixture until well coated.

Spread the zucchini over the puff pastry base. Bake the veggie galette for 18–20 minutes, until the pastry is crisp and golden and the zucchini is cooked.

Remove the galette from the oven and slice into portions. Serve immediately with the rest of your supper menu while still crisp and hot.

PREP TIP

This galette tastes best when freshly baked, but you can prepare the vegetables the previous day. If you are short of time and don't mind a slight compromise on the finished result, the galette itself can also be baked in advance.

flatbreads with black cumin

¾ cup (200 mL) lukewarm water

7 tbsp (100 mL) dark beer

⅓ ounce (10 g) fresh yeast

3⅓ cups (400 g) organic all-purpose flour

1¼ tsp (8 g) sea salt, plus more to serve

2 tbsp black cumin seeds

7 tbsp (100 mL) olive oil, for frying

Combine the water and beer in a bowl. Crumble in the yeast and stir to dissolve. Stir in a bit of flour, then stir in the salt. Now, add the rest of the flour and mix vigorously with a wooden spoon to create a smooth and elastic dough. Lift the spoon repeatedly through the mixture until the dough comes away from the sides of the bowl.

Cover the dough with a kitchen towel and leave to prove at room temperature for about 1 hour, until doubled in volume.

Divide the dough into 8–10 pieces on a floured work surface. Press or roll the pieces of dough to make flatbreads, and sprinkle them with the black cumin seeds.

Heat a couple tbsp of the olive oil to a high temperature in a large non-stick skillet. Fry a few flatbreads (depending on the size of your skillet) for 1–2 minutes on each side, until they are browned and crisp. Repeat with the remaining oil and rolled-out dough pieces.

Sprinkle the flatbreads with sea salt while they are still warm, and use them to dip, dunk, and scoop your various supper dishes.

PREP TIP

Make the flatbread dough the previous day (up to the point where it has been left to prove and has doubled in volume), then store it covered in the fridge. Fry the flatbreads before your guests arrive, and reheat them on a hotplate or under the broiler just before serving.

spinach salad with dates, pomegranate, and crunchy chickpeas

SERVES 4

Timing: Start the previous day.

1 cup (200 g) dried chickpeas
1 tsp fennel seeds
1 tsp ground cumin
1 tsp dried chili flakes
1 pomegranate
2 oz (50 g) Medjool dates
2 organic lemons
1 tsp acacia honey
Sea salt
Freshly ground black pepper
7 tbsp (100 mL) olive oil
18 oz (500 g) baby spinach

Soak the chickpeas in a bowl with plenty of cold water for 24 hours. The next day, drain the chickpeas, place them in a pan with fresh water, and bring to a boil. Then, lower the temperature and simmer for about 30 minutes, until the beans are tender. Remove the pan from the heat, let the chickpeas sit in the pan for a few more minutes, then drain.

Toast the fennel seeds, ground cumin, and chili flakes in a dry pan until they are popping gently and releasing their aroma. Grind the toasted spices with a mortar and pestle (or in a spice grinder) to create a fine powder.

Slice the pomegranate in half crosswise, hold the cut surface over a bowl, and tap the skin vigorously with a spoon to knock the seeds out into the bowl. Pit and finely chop the dates.

Zest and juice the lemons. Combine the lemon zest and juice with the honey, a pinch of salt, and a few grinds of black pepper in a bowl. Gradually whisk in 3 tbsp of the olive oil until you have a smooth and creamy dressing. Taste and add more salt and pepper as desired.

Heat 2 tbsp of the remaining olive oil in a skillet over a moderate temperature and fry the chickpeas for 3–5 minutes, tossing regularly, until they are golden yellow and crisp. Stir in a pinch of salt, ground spices, and the remaining 2 tbsp of olive oil until the chickpeas are coated in the spices. Transfer the chickpeas to a bowl.

Toss together the spinach, dates, pomegranate seeds, and dressing in a large bowl, then transfer the salad mixture to a serving dish. Scatter the lukewarm, crunchy chickpeas over the salad. Serve with the other midweek supper recipes while the spinach has not yet completely wilted and the chickpeas are still nice and crisp.

PREP TIP
The chickpeas can be cooked the previous day and stored in the cooking liquid. However, they should not be toasted until just before your supper.

raita with cucumber, pickled red onions, and mint

SERVES 4

1 red onion
Sea salt
2 tbsp cider vinegar
1 tbsp acacia honey
2 mini cucumbers
½ cup (100 g) yogurt
Freshly ground black pepper
10 sprigs mint

Peel and finely chop the red onion, then combine with a pinch of salt, cider vinegar, and acacia honey in a bowl. Massage the ingredients with your hands until the onions soften slightly and absorb some of the honey and vinegar.

Peel the cucumbers, slice in half lengthwise, and scrape out the seeds with a spoon. Roughly chop the cucumbers and toss them in the onion mixture.

Stir in the yogurt, then season the raita to taste with additional salt and freshly ground pepper.

Strip the mint leaves from the stalks. Chop the leaves and stir half of them into the raita. Transfer the raita to a serving dish and garnish with the remaining chopped mint leaves.

Serve as a wonderfully refreshing component to go with the other mid-week supper dishes.

PREP TIP
Why not get one of your guests to help you prepare this dish!

roasted onions with oranges and buttermilk dressing

6 medium onions

7 tbsp (100 mL) buttermilk

2 organic blood oranges

Sea salt

4 tbsp (60 mL) olive oil

1 tsp whole pink peppercorns

1 tbsp buckwheat, to garnish

Preheat the oven to 320°F (160°C).

Roast the unpeeled onions in a baking dish for 1 hour or until they are really soft. Remove the onions from the oven and let them cool slightly.

Season the buttermilk in a bowl with the zest of 1 blood orange, a pinch of sea salt, and 2 tbsp of the olive oil. Stir the buttermilk dressing well.

Peel and segment both the blood oranges, finely chop the segments, and transfer to a bowl. Roughly crush the pink peppercorns and add these to the fruit.

Slice the tops and bottoms off the roasted onions, then peel and quarter them. Split the quarters into segments, arrange these segments in a little serving bowl, and scatter with the diced orange. Drizzle with the buttermilk dressing and the remaining 2 tbsp of olive oil and serve alongside the other midweek supper dishes.

PREP TIP
You can roast the onions the weekend before your supper and keep them in their skins in the fridge.

spicy roasted pepper salsa

SERVES 4

3 red bell peppers

2 tomatoes

1 red chili pepper

1 garlic clove

7 tbsp (100 mL) olive oil

Sea salt

Freshly ground black pepper

¾ cup (100 g) almonds

2 tbsp sherry vinegar

Preheat the oven to 400°F (200°C).

Halve the bell peppers, remove the membranes and seeds, and transfer to an ovenproof dish.

Roughly dice the tomatoes and add them to the dish with the halved bell peppers, along with the whole chili and garlic clove. Drizzle with 1 tbsp of the olive oil. Season to taste with salt and pepper.

Roast the bell peppers for 20–25 minutes, until they are slightly soft and browning nicely. Remove the dish from the oven and leave to cool slightly.

Toast the almonds in a dry pan, then season lightly with salt.

Purée the roasted peppers with the remaining 6 tbsp of olive oil and sherry vinegar using a food processor or hand blender. Season to taste with salt and pepper.

Serve the salsa as a dip with your supper—it goes beautifully with any of the dishes from this menu.

PREP TIP

Make the salsa the weekend before your supper and store in the fridge. Remove from the fridge an hour or so before serving to ensure that it comes to room temperature.

whole roasted
tahini cauliflower

SERVES 4

1 head cauliflower

2 tbsp olive oil

Zest and juice of ½ organic lemon

Sea salt

Freshly ground black pepper

½ bunch common verbena (or mint)

1 oz (25 g) pistachios

1 tbsp ground sumac

TAHINI DRESSING

Zest and juice of 1 organic lemon

1 tsp dried chili flakes

Sea salt

2 tbsp tahini (sesame seed paste)

1 tsp acacia honey

3½ tbsp (50 mL) olive oil

Preheat the oven to 340°F (170°C).

Remove the outer green leaves from the cauliflower and rinse it under cold water. Place the whole cauliflower head in a baking dish, drizzle with the olive oil and lemon juice, and sprinkle with the lemon zest, a pinch of salt, and a few grinds of black pepper.

Bake the cauliflower for 30–35 minutes, until it is golden yellow and tender on the outside but still firm in the center. The best way to test it is by inserting a small knife: If the cauliflower is ready, the knife should go in easily. Remove the cauliflower from the oven and let it cool slightly.

Strip the verbena leaves from the stalks, chop the pistachios, and set both aside.

To make the tahini dressing, use a hand blender to blitz the lemon zest and juice, chili flakes, salt, tahini, honey, and 2 tbsp of water in a bowl until smooth. Stream in the olive oil while the blender is running to make a smooth and creamy dressing.

Break the roasted cauliflower into rough chunks and arrange these on a deep serving plate. Drizzle with tahini dressing and sprinkle with pistachios, verbena, and ground sumac.

Serve the cauliflower lukewarm or at room temperature along with the other midweek supper recipes.

PREP TIP

The cauliflower can be prepared the previous day and initially left whole. You can also make the tahini dressing in advance. Store both in the fridge, then let them come to room temperature before your guests arrive.

poached pears with spiced ice cream

SERVES 4–8

Requires: Ice cream maker

Timing: Allow enough time for the ice cream to infuse and freeze.

POACHED PEARS

1½ cups (300 g) sugar

7 tbsp (100 mL) cider vinegar

1 cinnamon stick

2 star anise pods

5 whole black peppercorns

3 bay leaves

4 small pears

1 organic orange

2 tbsp olive oil, for serving

SPICED ICE CREAM

3 oz (80 g) runny honey

6 egg yolks

1¾ cups (400 mL) heavy whipping cream

1¼ cups (300 mL) milk

Pinch of grated tonka bean

1 star anise pod

1 cinnamon stick

5 whole black peppercorns

2 green cardamom pods

To make the poached pears, combine the sugar, cider vinegar, cinnamon stick, star anise, peppercorns, bay leaf, and 3¼ cups (800 mL) of water in a saucepan and bring to a boil over medium-high heat.

Peel the pears. You can leave the stalks on and use them to hold the pears as you peel them. Slice the peeled pears in half.

Peel and quarter the orange and add to the pan. Reduce the heat and let the mixture simmer for 1–2 minutes, then add the halved pears to the liquid, ensuring that they are completely covered. Depending on their ripeness, poach the pears for 10–15 minutes, until they are soft but still have a slight bite.

Remove the pan from the heat and transfer the pears and liquid to a bowl. Once again, the pears should be completely covered. Put the bowl in the fridge to let the pears cool completely.

To make the spiced ice cream, whisk the honey and egg yolks in a bowl until light and fluffy.

In a saucepan, combine the cream, milk, grated tonka bean, star anise, cinnamon stick, peppercorns, and cardamom and bring just to a boil, then immediately remove it from the heat. Gradually stream this creamy mixture into the egg yolks, stirring constantly and whisking vigorously until the mixture thickens. Do not allow the mixture to get too hot or it will curdle.

Leave the ice cream mixture to stand at room temperature for 30–45 minutes to allow the cream to be infused by the spices.

Strain the mixture to remove the solid ingredients, then leave to cool. Next, transfer the mixture to an ice cream maker for processing until it is partially frozen and wonderfully creamy.

Tip the ice cream into a freezer container. Store in the freezer until ready to use.

For each serving, place 1–2 pear halves in a little bowl, pour over some of the poaching liquid, and top with a scoop of spiced ice cream. Drizzle with olive oil and serve immediately as a delicious end to an exquisite supper.

PREP TIP

The pears can be poached the previous weekend and left to infuse in the cooking liquid. You can also make the ice cream mixture 1–2 days ahead of time (don't make it too far in advance, due to the egg yolks). Keep the mixture in the fridge until a couple of hours before your guests are due, then process as described in your ice cream maker.

TIP

Why not make a large quantity of the pears and keep them in the fridge? If covered in the poaching liquid, the pears will keep for 3–4 weeks and become even more aromatic as time goes by.

midweek supper — menu planning and preparation

Inviting friends over to enjoy a delicious meal during the week is such a wonderful thing, and—with a bit of planning—you can pull off an evening's hosting with no stress at all. You should definitely prepare as much as you can the day before, or even the previous weekend, so that once your guests arrive there are just a few final things to deal with. Some people will no doubt be very happy to contribute one or two dishes themselves, or will come round beforehand to help you get ready. We recommend putting all the dishes out on the table at the same time, like at a buffet, so you can relax and eat together.

THE PREVIOUS WEEKEND OR
A FEW DAYS IN ADVANCE

HIBISCUS JUICE (P. 129)
HOMEMADE GINGER BEER (P. 130)
Make the hibiscus juice and ginger beer the previous weekend to allow their full flavors to develop.

VEGGIE CHICKPEA TAGINE WITH
COCONUT MILK AND MINT (P. 132)
Make the tagine the previous weekend or a couple of days in advance to ensure a more rounded flavor. Remember, you will need to soak the chickpeas for 24 hours.

SPINACH SALAD WITH DATES, POMEGRANATE,
AND CRUNCHY CHICKPEAS (P. 142)
Soak the chickpeas a few days in advance, replacing the water daily. You can also cook them the previous day and store them in their cooking liquid, but don't toast them until just before your guests arrive.

ROASTED ONIONS WITH ORANGE
AND BUTTERMILK DRESSING (P. 146)
Roast the onions the previous weekend and store them in the fridge. Before your guests arrive, peel the onions and prepare the rest of the recipe.

SPICY ROASTED PEPPER SALSA (P. 149)

Make the salsa the previous weekend and store in the fridge. Remove from the fridge in plenty of time to bring the dish to room temperature before serving.

POACHED PEARS WITH SPICED ICE CREAM (P. 153)

Poach the pears the weekend before your supper and let them infuse in the cooking liquid. If covered in the poaching liquid, they will keep for 3–4 weeks in the fridge and will become even more aromatic as time goes by.

THE PREVIOUS DAY

VEGGIE GALETTE WITH HERBS AND PARMESAN (P. 138)

This galette can be baked the previous day and reheated. However, it's even better to prepare the vegetables ahead of time and bake the galette itself to be eaten fresh when your guests arrive.

FLATBREADS WITH BLACK CUMIN (P. 141)

Make the dough for the flatbreads the previous day and store in the fridge.

WHOLE ROASTED TAHINI CAULIFLOWER (P. 150)

Roast the cauliflower, leaving it whole. Prepare the tahini dressing, and store both components, covered, in the fridge. Remove the cauliflower and dressing from the fridge a few hours before your guests are due because you want the food to be at room temperature to serve.

POACHED PEARS WITH SPICED ICE CREAM (P. 153)

Make the ice cream mixture no more than 1–2 days in advance, due to the egg yolks, and keep in the fridge. Freeze the mixture using an ice cream maker a couple of hours before your guests are due.

ON THE DAY ITSELF

FLATBREADS WITH BLACK CUMIN (P. 141)

Cook the flatbreads before your guests arrive, then reheat them briefly under the broiler when ready to serve.

M'HAMSA WITH PRESERVED LEMON, CHILI, RHUBARB, AND PARSLEY (P. 136)

Why not delegate the task of making the m'hamsa to one of your guests? They could join you in the kitchen an hour before everyone arrives or cook this item the previous day to bring with them.

RAITA WITH CUCUMBER, PICKLED RED ONIONS, AND MINT (P. 144)

Make the raita just before serving—this is a task you could assign to one of your guests.

christmas dinner

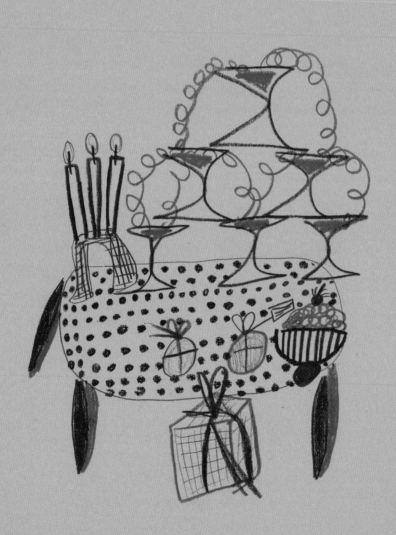

Christmas Eve is a time of huge anticipation in my family and a day for cherished traditions. As you might expect, the absolute highlight is the festive evening meal with the extended family.

Preparations for the duck and crispy roast pork begin early in the morning—both dishes are an essential part of a typical Danish Christmas meal. At some point we grab breakfast, and the family makes Christmas decorations. The morning is all about hygge, while the smell of Christmas dinner gradually permeates the air.

After a light lunch, we go to church, where we meet other relatives and enjoy listening to the Copenhagen Boys' Choir. Once the service is over, we head outside to enjoy a glass of port and a few Christmas cookies that we've brought with us. Then, there is time for a short nap before we get dressed up at about 6 pm for Christmas dinner, which always involves a big gathering of people.

The festivities kick off with a small appetizer and a glass of champagne, then comes a lavish feast that usually lasts several hours. Finally, we dance around the Christmas tree, unwrap the gifts, and devour huge quantities of cookies. The lovely, long evening eventually comes to a close, and we fall happily into bed.

The following menu is based on my family's favorite dishes and traditions. You can either cook the entire thing or pick individual components that take your fancy, depending on your own festive customs. As always, I hope you have a wonderful time enjoying delicious food surrounded by your favorite people!

163

hot apple punch
with spices

MAKES 6–8 GLASSES
(EACH ROUGHLY ⅔ CUP/150 ML)

4¼ cups (1 L) unsweetened cloudy apple
    juice (homemade if available)

2 apples, 1 thinly sliced, 1 diced

Juice of ½ lemon

2 tbsp raw cane sugar

1 (0.2-in/½-cm-thick) slice organic ginger

1 cinnamon stick

2 star anise pods

5 whole black peppercorns

5 bay leaves

Bring all the ingredients except the diced apple to a boil in a saucepan, remove from the heat, and let infuse for 30–60 minutes at room temperature.

Reheat again gently and, if necessary, adjust the flavor with additional lemon juice and ginger.

Just before serving, strain the punch through a sieve and add the freshly diced apple.

This refreshing hot drink is the perfect prelude to the celebratory Christmas feast and can be enjoyed while you finish off the final preparations. It is also a great option to warm yourself up again after a woodland walk on a cold winter's day.

PREP TIP
The apple punch can be started the previous day; if left to infuse overnight, the spices and ginger will impart a particularly intense flavor.

oysters with horseradish vinaigrette

SERVES 6

1 apple
1–2 tbsp (5–10 g) peeled and grated
  fresh horseradish root
3½ tbsp (50 mL) extra-virgin olive oil
3½ tbsp (50 mL) cider vinegar
Freshly ground black pepper
12 fresh oysters
¼ bunch chives (optional)

Core the apple and dice it very finely. In a bowl, combine the diced apple with the horseradish, olive oil, cider vinegar, and some freshly ground pepper; whisk to make a smooth vinaigrette.

Scrub the oyster shells thoroughly. To open the oysters, first take a kitchen towel and fold it to make a thick rectangle. Place an oyster curved-side down on one end of the towel, and fold the other end of the towel over the shell. This helps protect the hand holding the oyster.

Carefully insert the tip of an oyster knife or other small, sturdy knife just inside the shell's "hinge." Press the blade of the knife down, then twist to pry open the shell. Run the knife around the top shell to remove it. Check that the oysters are fresh (they should have a fresh, salty smell and the liquid should be clear), then use the knife to separate the oyster from the lower shell, removing any broken bits of shell if necessary.

Arrange the shells on a serving dish, making sure the water is retained in the bottom halves with the oysters. Drizzle each oyster lightly with vinaigrette. Finely chop the chives (if using) and scatter over the oysters.

Serve immediately as an appetizer before Christmas dinner. A glass of champagne is the perfect accompaniment to raise a toast.

duck confit

SERVES 6

Timing: Start the previous day.

6 duck legs
1 tbsp flaked sea salt
½ bunch thyme
5 garlic cloves
6–7 bay leaves
1 tbsp whole black peppercorns
2¼ pounds (1 kg) duck fat
Coarse sea salt

The day before, put the duck legs in a roasting pan or ovenproof dish along with the salt flakes, thyme, whole garlic cloves, bay leaves, and peppercorns. Carefully rub the seasoning into the meat. Cover the roasting pan and refrigerate overnight.

The following day, preheat the oven to 285°F (140°C).

Remove the duck legs from the roasting pan, dab off any excess salt, and return the legs to the pan. Add the duck fat and roast for 2 hours.

The meat should be very tender. If not, cover the duck and continue roasting for another 30 minutes.

Remove the duck legs from the oven and leave to cool in the fat. Alternatively, you can proceed immediately to fry the legs as follows:

To finish the duck, remove the legs from the fat and fry them skin-side down in a skillet until nicely crisp. Turn each piece over and fry for another couple of minutes until beautifully crisp on both sides.

Sprinkle lightly with sea salt and serve with the Christmas Gravy (p. 174) and other Christmas dinner dishes.

TIP

Heat any leftover fat in a saucepan until completely melted, then pour through a sieve into a sterilized screw-top jar. Keep this fat in the fridge until the next time you want to make confit de canard. It is also the perfect ingredient to make delicious roast potatoes.

PREP TIP

You can easily make the duck legs 3–4 days before Christmas. Just keep them in the cooking fat in the fridge.

crispy roast pork with bay leaves and sea salt

SERVES 6

2¼ lbs (1 kg) Boston butt (pork shoulder) with skin (bone-in, if desired)

Coarse sea salt

10–15 bay leaves

Freshly ground black pepper

Preheat the oven to 350°F (180°C).

Use a sharp knife to make lots of crosswise scores in the skin, spacing them 0.2 inch (5 mm) apart (see photo). Make sure you do not pierce the meat underneath.

Sprinkle the skin with plenty of coarse salt, moisten your hands with water, and massage the salt into the skin. The water ensures that the salt adheres to the fat. This also makes the skin sizzle as soon as it is cooked and produces wonderfully crisp cracklings.

Insert the bay leaves in the incisions in the pork skin, then place the meat skin-side up on a metal roasting rack. Suspend the rack over a pan to catch the fat and roast for 65–70 minutes, until the skin is crisp. Remove from the oven and let rest for 10–15 minutes.

If desired, you can cut the meat off the bone before serving, then slice and season with pepper. Serve with the Christmas Gravy (p. 174) and other Christmas dinner dishes.

PREP TIP

You can score and salt the skin in the morning. You can even roast the pork around midday until cooked, then simply reheat for 15–20 minutes before the meal in the evening.

christmas gravy

SERVES 6

8½ cups (2 L) duck stock or
   rich chicken stock
1 tbsp duck fat
2 tbsp all-purpose flour
1 tbsp cider vinegar
1 tsp sugar
Sea salt
Freshly ground black pepper

Boil the stock in a saucepan over high heat until reduced by roughly a quarter. Remove from the heat and let the duck fat melt in the hot liquid. The fat will separate and settle on the surface.

Sift the flour into the pan and slowly let it be absorbed by the fat on the surface. Then, use a balloon whisk to beat everything together while you bring the pan to a boil (the flour helps bind everything; the fat gives the gravy a lovely duck flavor). If any excess fat still settles on the surface, scoop it away.

Adjust the consistency of the gravy if required. To create a thicker gravy that will stick to the potatoes, add some more flour and cook for another 5 minutes.

Season the gravy with the cider vinegar, sugar, and salt and pepper to taste. Serve hot with the rest of your Christmas dinner.

boiled potatoes

SERVES 6

2¼ lbs (1 kg) waxy potatoes
Sea salt
1 tbsp butter

Wash the potatoes briefly in cold water, then transfer to a saucepan and cover with fresh cold water. Add a generous handful of salt and slowly bring to a boil with the lid on. Scoop off any white foam or other impurities from the surface of the water, and continue boiling the potatoes for 10 minutes over moderate heat.

Remove the pan from the heat and leave the potatoes in their cooking liquid for 10 minutes or until they are tender.

Drain the potatoes, immerse them briefly in cold water, and peel off the skins.

To serve, reheat the potatoes in the pan with the butter and some salt.

PREP TIP
You can also cook and peel the potatoes the previous day. Store them in the fridge and reheat briefly just before serving. Make a double quantity of boiled potatoes, then keep half of them for making Caramelized Potatoes (p. 176).

caramelized potatoes

SERVES 6

2¼ lbs (1 kg) small waxy potatoes
½ cup (100 g) sugar
1¾ tbsp (25 g) butter

Cook and peel the potatoes as described in the Boiled Potatoes recipe (p. 175).

Measure the sugar into a heavy-bottomed skillet, put it over medium heat, and cook without stirring until it turns golden brown and begins to caramelize. Add the butter and let this melt, stirring occasionally, until you have a smooth caramel mixture.

Carefully toss the peeled boiled potatoes in the caramel, ensuring that they are well coated. Cook the potatoes for a few minutes in the caramel until they have browned nicely. Remove the potatoes from the skillet while they are still firm in the middle and retaining their shape.

These caramelized potatoes go particularly well with the rich Duck Confit (p. 168), but they also make a great accompaniment for any of the other Christmas dinner recipes.

PREP TIP
Cook and peel the potatoes the previous day and keep them in the fridge. Caramelize the potatoes just before you are ready to serve.

raw red cabbage salad with dried fruits, orange, and walnuts

SERVES 6

¼ head red cabbage
   (roughly 10 oz/300 g)
2 oz (50 g) dried figs
1 oz (25 g) dates
1 organic orange
2 tbsp cider vinegar
3 tbsp olive oil
1 tbsp runny honey
Sea salt
Freshly ground black pepper
1 oz (25 g) walnuts

Grate the red cabbage into a serving bowl. Chop the dried fruit into little pieces and mix with the red cabbage.

Finely zest the orange. In a bowl, whisk the orange zest with the cider vinegar, olive oil, honey, and salt and pepper to taste to make the dressing.

Peel and segment the orange, then dice the flesh and stir it into the dressing.

Pour the dressing over the red cabbage and toss well.

Finely chop the walnuts and mix them into the salad. Make sure everything is well combined, then serve with the Duck Confit (p. 168) and other Christmas dinner dishes.

PREP TIP
You can prepare the individual components for this salad a few hours ahead of time, but don't add the dressing or walnuts until just before you are ready to serve to make sure everything stays nice and crisp.

red cabbage with orange, cinnamon, and star anise

SERVES 6

1 red cabbage

2 organic oranges

3 cinnamon sticks

5 star anise pods

4 bay leaves

¾ cup (120 g) raw cane sugar

1¼ cups (300 mL) red currant or black currant juice (ideally unsweetened)

¾ cup (200 mL) cherry vinegar (or other dark fruit vinegar)

1¾ cups (400 mL) red wine

1 tbsp sea salt

Split the red cabbage into quarters, remove the tough core, and grate it into a saucepan.

Roughly chop the oranges, including their rinds, remove any seeds, and add to the pan along with the remaining ingredients.

Cover the pan with a lid and bring everything to a boil. Then, lower the temperature and simmer for 1–1½ hours with the lid on. The cabbage is ready when it has absorbed most of the liquid and has a lovely, glossy appearance.

Serve as a fruity side dish to go with your festive Christmas meal.

PREP TIP

You can cook the red cabbage the previous day and keep it in the fridge overnight to allow the flavors to develop. Reheat the dish before serving.

danish rice pudding with cherry sauce

RICE PUDDING
2 cups (500 mL) milk
⅓ cup (65 g) short-grain rice
½ vanilla pod
Salt
1¼ cups (300 mL) heavy whipping cream
¾ cup (100 g) blanched almonds
¼ cup (25 g) powdered (icing) sugar
Zest of ½ organic lemon

CHERRY SAUCE
2 organic oranges
⅓ cup (65 g) superfine (caster) sugar
1 (14-oz/400-g) jar Morello cherries
7 tbsp (100 mL) Danish cherry wine
   (kirsebærvin)
1 star anise pod
1 tsp cornstarch

To make the rice pudding, bring the milk to a boil in a heavy-bottomed saucepan, then stir in the rice. Adjust the temperature so the milk is barely simmering.

Scrape out the seeds from the vanilla pod half and set them aside. Add the pod (from which you have just scraped the seeds) and some salt to milk and rice. Stir and continue simmering the rice over low heat for 45–50 minutes, stirring occasionally, until tender. Transfer the rice pudding to a bowl and leave to cool.

For the cherry sauce, grate the zest from half of one of the oranges. Squeeze the juice from both oranges into a small saucepan, add the orange zest, sugar, cherries and cherry juice from the jar, the cherry wine, star anise, and 7 tbsp (100 mL) of water and bring to a boil. Simmer everything for 2–3 minutes.

In a small bowl, stir the cornstarch into some cold water until smooth. Gradually add this mixture to the sauce, stirring constantly, until it has thickened slightly. Remove the pan from the heat and test the flavor of the cherry sauce; it should have a good balance between sweet and sour components. Keep the cherry sauce warm until ready to serve.

Gently whip the cream in a bowl and add the reserved vanilla seeds. Roughly chop the almonds and fold these into the cooled rice pudding, along with the cream. Add the powdered sugar and lemon zest.

To serve, drizzle each portion of rice pudding with 1 tbsp of cherry sauce (or more if desired).

PREP TIP
You can make the rice pudding the previous day and keep it in the fridge. Fold in the almonds and cream just before serving. The cherry sauce can also be made the day before. Cover and keep in the fridge, then reheat just before serving.

jødekager cookies

MAKES 80–100 COOKIES

Timing: Allow 2 hours for the dough to rest.

1 cup + 2 tbsp (250 g) butter, at room
   temperature
1½ cups (300 g) sugar
1 tsp salt
2 eggs
2¾ cups (340 g) all-purpose flour
1 tsp baking powder

TOPPING
2 tbsp sugar
1 tsp ground cinnamon

Process the butter, sugar, and salt in a food processor until smooth. Add the eggs, one at a time, and mix until thoroughly combined. Scrape the mixture into a large bowl and gradually fold in the flour, using a wooden spoon.

In a small bowl, dissolve the baking powder in 1 tsp boiling water. Then, work this into the cookie dough until evenly distributed.

Shape the dough into long sausages (¾–1 inch/2–3 cm in diameter). Wrap each piece in parchment paper and refrigerate for a couple of hours, until the dough is firm enough to cut into slices.

Preheat the oven to 340°F (170°C) (convection setting). Line a large baking sheet with parchment paper.

Unwrap the dough and slice into very thin circles. Arrange the cookies on the prepared baking sheet, spacing them about 1 inch (2.5 cm) apart. Combine the sugar and cinnamon in a small bowl and sprinkle over the cookies.

Bake the cookies for 7–10 minutes, until crisp and golden. Cool slightly on a wire rack. They taste particularly good if eaten fresh and warm while they still have a lovely, crumbly texture.

TIP
Just bake however many cookies you want, and keep the rest of the dough in the fridge (for up to 4 days) or freezer (for up to 1 month).

brunkager cookies

MAKES 35 COOKIES

¼ cup (60 g) butter

⅓ cup (75 g) muscovado sugar
   (or fine raw cane sugar)

5 oz (145 g) molasses (or treacle)

2 tsp fresh orange zest

1 tsp ground cinnamon

½ tsp ground cloves

½ tsp ground ginger

Zest of 1 organic lemon

1 tsp culinary potash (or ¾ tsp baking soda)

2 cups + 1 tbsp (250 g) all-purpose flour,
   plus more to work with

2 tbsp roughly chopped blanched almonds

Combine the butter, sugar, and syrup in a pan and bring to a boil. Stir in the orange zest, cinnamon, cloves, ginger, and lemon zest. Remove the pan from the heat.

Stir the potash into a small quantity of cold water in a bowl until smooth, then stir this mixture into the hot syrup. Leave the syrup to cool completely.

Pour the cooled syrup into a large bowl, then use a wooden spoon to stir in the flour a little at a time. When all the flour is incorporated, knead the mixture by hand until a smooth dough forms.

Preheat the oven to 340°F (170°C) (convection setting). Line a large baking sheet with parchment paper.

Roll out the cookie dough on a floured work surface, and use a dough wheel to slice it into diamonds or whatever shapes you prefer. Transfer the cookies to the prepared baking sheet and put a piece of almond in the center of each one.

Bake the cookies for 7–8 minutes, until they darken slightly and become a bit crisp, then transfer to a wire rack and allow to cool.

TIP
If wrapped in aluminum foil, the raw cookie dough will keep in the fridge for several days. Store the baked cookies in an airtight container.

finskbrød cookies

MAKES 50 COOKIES

Timing: Allow 1 hour to chill the dough.

2¾ cups (325 g) all-purpose flour
½ cup (100 g) sugar
1 cup + 2 tbsp (250 g) butter
Pinch of salt

TOPPING
1 egg
1 cup (150 g) almonds
3 tbsp pearl sugar

Combine the flour and sugar in a mixing bowl. Dice the butter and rub this into the flour and sugar with the salt to make a short cookie dough. Use plastic wrap to cover the dough, and chill in the fridge for 1 hour.

Preheat the oven to 345°F (175°C) (convection setting). Line a large baking sheet with parchment paper.

For the topping, whisk the egg in a deep dish.

Roughly chop the almonds in a food processor, then tip these into another deep dish.

Pour the pearl sugar into a third dish.

Divide the dough into 5 equal pieces. Shape each piece into a long, roughly 1-inch/2½-cm thick strand, then flatten each slightly with the blade of a knife and cut into 10 equal pieces. You will have 50 pieces total when you are done cutting all the dough.

Dip the top of each cookie into the egg, then the almonds, and finally the pearl sugar. Arrange the cookies on the prepared baking sheet, spacing them about 1 inch (2 cm) apart.

Bake the cookies for 15 minutes or until they are browning slightly. If they are still too pale, continue baking for 3 minutes. Allow the cookies to cool briefly on a wire rack.

These make a fantastic snack or could be served with Hot Apple Punch (p. 160) as a treat after an afternoon walk on a freezing cold winter's day.

TIP
Store the cookies in an airtight container.

vanilla shortbread cookies

MAKES 50 COOKIES

Timing: Allow 2 hours for the dough to rest.

5½ cups (50 g) whole unsalted almonds
1 vanilla pod
½ cup (100 g) sugar
2 cups + 1 tbsp (250 g) all-purpose flour
Pinch of baking powder
¾ cup + 1 tbsp (190 g) butter
Pinch of salt
1 egg

Finely chop the almonds.

Slice the vanilla pod lengthwise, scrape the seeds into a small bowl, and add a small amount of the sugar; use your fingers to rub the vanilla beans into the sugar. This technique ensures that the vanilla seeds will be distributed better through the cookie dough.

In a large bowl, combine the vanilla sugar, flour, remaining plain sugar, baking powder, chopped almonds, butter, and salt. Knead by hand to create the dough. Finally, work in the egg until it is fully incorporated. Cover the bowl with plastic wrap and let the dough rest for a couple of hours in the fridge.

Preheat the oven to 350°F (180°C) (convection setting). Line a large baking sheet with parchment paper.

Fit a piping bag with the star nozzle. Fill the bag with cookie dough, then pipe the dough into roughly 4-inch/10-cm-long ropes. Shape these ropes into rings and arrange them on the prepared baking sheet.

Bake the vanilla cookies for about 8 minutes or until golden brown, then transfer to a wire rack to cool briefly. These cookies taste fantastic with an afternoon coffee during the Christmas festivities.

TIP
Store the cookies in an airtight container.

christmas dinner — menu planning and preparation

Christmas Eve is a time to be with family, although close friends are welcome too, of course. Spending time relaxing with loved ones and celebrating with your own special traditions is the highlight of winter for many people. Everyone looks forward so much to the evening festivities, and the process of getting ready is all part of the fun. Activities include making Christmas decorations, decorating the tree, and of course getting various dishes ready for the Christmas dinner. With the right planning, there should be plenty of time for rest and relaxation.

THE PREVIOUS WEEK

COOKIE BAKING
Most of the cookies (pp. 187–194) can be made in the run up to Christmas or at least a few days before the main event. Just store them in airtight containers. If you have a habit of nibbling at the supplies, you might need to bake a second batch so you don't run out on Christmas Eve.

THE PREVIOUS DAY

HOT APPLE PUNCH WITH SPICES (P. 160)
Make the apple punch the previous day so the flavor of the spices and ginger can develop fully.

DUCK CONFIT (P. 168)
Season the duck legs the previous day (or even a few days in advance) and keep in the refrigerator to be cooked the following day.

RED CABBAGE WITH ORANGE, CINNAMON, AND STAR ANISE (P. 182)
Cook the red cabbage the previous day and keep in the fridge overnight. Reheat before serving.

BOILED POTATOES (P. 175);
CARAMELIZED POTATOES (P. 176)

Cook and peel the potatoes the previous day and store in the fridge. On Christmas Eve, caramelize one half and reheat the other half in a pan with some butter and salt.

DANISH RICE PUDDING WITH CHERRY SAUCE (P. 184)

Cook the rice for this dessert the previous day and refrigerate. Then, all you have to do on the day itself is fold in the almonds and cream. The cherry sauce can also be made a day in advance and reheated before serving.

ON THE DAY ITSELF

DUCK CONFIT (P. 168)

Ideally, cook the seasoned duck legs in the morning. They can be left to cool in the fat, then fried when you are ready to serve so they are nice and crisp. You can even prepare the duck legs 3–4 days in advance; just keep them in the fridge in the fat.

CRISPY ROAST PORK WITH BAY LEAVES
AND SEA SALT (P. 173)

In the morning, prepare the meat by making incisions in the skin and seasoning with salt. If you like, you can even cook the roast at midday. All you have to do in the evening is reheat it for 15–20 minutes.

RAW RED CABBAGE SALAD WITH DRIED FRUITS,
ORANGE, AND WALNUTS (P. 181)

You can prepare this salad a few hours in advance; just add the dressing and walnuts when you are ready to serve to ensure that it stays beautifully crisp.

FINAL ARRANGEMENTS

All the family can easily join in the final arrangements in the evening. It's great fun rustling up a batch of cookies together, or sliding the roast into the oven, chopping the final few ingredients for the red cabbage salad, and discussing the tree decorations all while sipping some apple punch.

birthday picnic

My wife Camilla and I have always loved celebrating birthdays. When we first got to know each other, Camilla used to celebrate her birthday twice a year! So, for the first few years we always had an additional celebration in May—we didn't do gifts the second time round, but there would definitely be delicious food, better weather than in November, and an added dose of Danish hygge.

Ever since the birth of our first son, Oscar, and his three siblings, Alma, Konrad, and Viggo, we have tried to make our children's birthdays really special occasions. We start with an early morning rendition of "Happy Birthday," then there is a birthday breakfast with gifts, and the day is rounded off with an evening meal featuring the birthday child's favorite food. Finally, the following weekend, we invite friends and family over for an afternoon of fun and games with cakes, snacks, and everything else that belongs to a successful children's birthday party.

In this section, I've collected some of the recipes that we often made on these occasions. Kids and adults alike love these delicious treats, which offer plenty of variety and interest for your birthday spread. Many of the dishes can be made for a picnic and enjoyed outdoors. These are tried and tested favorites that taste absolutely fantastic and capture the essence of what is surely the best day of the year!

raspberry soda
with verbena

MAKES 10–12 (½-CUP/
125-ML) GLASSES

1 organic lemon

1 lemongrass stalk

5½ cups (700 g) raspberries
   (fresh or frozen)

1 cup (200 g) sugar

4¼ cups (1 L) sparkling
   mineral water

Ice cubes

Leaves from 5 sprigs
   common verbena

Quarter the lemon, bash the lemongrass, and chop both into little pieces. Add to a pan with the raspberries, sugar, and 2 cups (500 mL) of water. (If using frozen berries, reduce the water by about ⅓ cup/80 mL.) Bring to a boil. Simmer everything for 5–7 minutes, until you have a creamy syrup. Remove from the heat and leave to cool completely.

Strain the cooled berry mixture through a sieve into a bowl. Press the raspberries left in the sieve with a wooden spoon to extract as much liquid as possible.

Combine the strained fruit syrup and mineral water in a decanter or jug and add ice cubes.

Place a couple of verbena leaves in each glass, then pour in the raspberry soda.

Serve immediately as a refreshing welcome drink.

PREP TIP
You can prepare the raspberry juice a couple of days in advance. The flavor will be enhanced by being left to infuse in the fridge. Only add the mineral water and ice cubes just before serving.

candy-topped
birthday buns

MAKES 20–25 BUNS

Timing: Allow up to 3½ hours proving time for the dough.

2½ oz (70 g) fresh yeast

3 eggs

8½ cups (1.25 kg) all-purpose flour,
    plus more as needed

⅔ cup (130 g) sugar

4¼ tsp (20 g) sea salt,
    plus more as needed

7 tbsp (100 g) butter

ICING

¾ cup (100 g) powdered (icing) sugar

TOPPING

2 handfuls assorted candies

Crumble the yeast into 2½ cups (600 mL) lukewarm water in the bowl of an electric mixer fitted with the dough hook; stir with a wooden spoon to dissolve. Add 2 of the eggs, one at a time, mixing well with the electric mixer before adding the next one. Add the flour, sugar, and salt, and use the electric mixer to knead the mixture on a low setting just until the dough comes away from the sides of the bowl.

Chop the butter into small cubes, sprinkle with a generous pinch of salt, then add it to the bowl with the dough; mix on low until the butter is incorporated and the dough is smooth and silky. Cover the bowl with a kitchen towel and let the dough rest at room temperature for 30 minutes.

Transfer the dough to a lightly floured work surface and shape into 20–25 balls. Line a large baking sheet with parchment paper. Place the little spheres of dough on the baking sheet and arrange them in any shape you like, leaving slight gaps in between; they will merge to form the desired shape as they rise. Cover the buns with a kitchen towel and leave to prove for 2–3 hours.

Preheat the oven to 400°F (200°C) (convection setting).

Whisk the remaining egg in a dish; use this to brush the buns. Bake for 10–12 minutes, until the tops of the buns are pale brown. Remove the buns from the oven and leave to cool.

Meanwhile, to make the icing, mix the powdered sugar with 2–3 tbsp lukewarm water until there are no lumps.

Dab the cooled buns with icing, then decorate with the candy. These buns also make attractive edible decorations for the gifts table!

PREP TIP
You can also make the yeast dough the previous evening, shape it into balls, then cover and leave to prove in the fridge.

rustic panini with cheese, mortadella, mustard, and basil

MAKES 4 PANINI

Requires: Panini press

8 slices sourdough bread
2 tbsp medium-hot mustard
1 (8-oz/227-g) ball fresh mozzarella
8 slices mortadella
Leaves from ½ bunch basil

Arrange the bread slices in pairs on a chopping board, and spread each one with a thin layer of mustard (use roughly ½ tbsp per pair).

Thinly slice the mozzarella and divide among 4 slices of bread. Top with mortadella and basil leaves. Top each sandwich with the remaining bread slices.

Finally, toast the panini in the panini press for 3–4 minutes, until each one is nice and crisp on the outside and the cheese is melting. (If you don't have a panini press, brush the outsides of the sandwiches with a little olive oil and toast them on a hot grill pan or heavy skillet for 2–3 minutes per side, until crisp and golden.)

Slice the pressed sandwiches into smaller pieces, and serve as soon as possible while the cheese is still hot and melted.

This delicious, savory snack is best served right at the start, before all the sweet treats are put out on the table.

PREP TIP
You can assemble the panini a few hours before your guests arrive and toast them shortly before serving.

wraps with egg salad, peas, and tarragon

SERVES 4

4 eggs

10 cornichons

½ cup (100 g) plain whole-fat yogurt

1 tsp curry powder

2 tbsp olive oil

Sea salt

Freshly ground black pepper

½ bunch tarragon

4 (8-inch / 20-cm) flour tortillas

¾ cup (100 g) fresh peas

Bring a pan of water to a boil, then cook the eggs for 8 minutes (so they are hard-boiled). Immerse the eggs in cold water to stop the cooking process, remove the shells, chop roughly, and transfer to a bowl.

Finely chop the cornichons. Carefully fold the yogurt, curry powder, olive oil, and cornichons into the eggs, making sure the pieces of egg retain their shape, then season to taste with salt and pepper.

Chop the tarragon. Put small scoops of egg salad on the flour tortillas, then scatter with the raw peas and chopped tarragon. Roll everything up to make tortilla wraps.

Slice the wraps in half and serve as a savory snack.

PREP TIP
You can make the egg salad the previous day and keep it in the fridge until ready to use.

raw summer vegetables
with sunflower seed dip

1¼ cups (150 g) sunflower seeds

1 tsp sea salt

3½ tbsp (50 mL) olive oil

2 tbsp cider vinegar

17½ oz (500 g) tender, crisp summer
vegetables (e.g. radishes, bunched carrots,
baby corn, fennel, cucumber)

Combine the sunflower seeds and salt in a small saucepan, then pour in just enough water to cover the seeds. Bring to a boil and cook the sunflower seeds for 15–20 minutes, until they are very soft and have absorbed most of the water.

Transfer the seeds and any remaining cooking water to a food processor, add the olive oil and vinegar, and purée until the consistency is smooth and creamy. Let the sunflower seed dip cool slightly in a bowl.

Carefully wash the summer vegetables. For radishes and bunched carrots, you may want to remove some of the greenery. Chop larger vegetables into sticks suitable for dipping.

Serve the crunchy vegetables with the sunflower seed dip.

PREP TIP
This dip can easily be prepared in advance. It will keep for 4–5 days in a sealed jar in the fridge (ideally covered with some olive oil to prevent discoloration).

rye toasts with ricotta and berries

SERVES 4

¼ loaf one-day-old rye bread

4 tbsp (60 mL) olive oil

1 tsp sea salt

¾ cup (200 g) ricotta

7 oz (200 g) mixed summer berries
  (e.g. red currants/black currants,
  raspberries, blackberries, gooseberries)

Preheat the oven to 300°F (150°C) (convection setting). Line a large baking sheet with parchment paper.

Use a sharp knife or a bread slicer to cut the rye bread into very thin slices. (Put the bread in the freezer for 20–30 minutes before slicing; this will make it easier to cut consistently thin slices.)

Place the slices of rye bread on the prepared baking sheet. Drizzle the bread with 2 tbsp of olive oil and sprinkle with sea salt. Bake the slices of bread for 8–10 minutes, until golden yellow and crisp. Do not let them go too dark or they will taste bitter.

Remove the toasted bread from the oven and leave to cool.

Scoop the ricotta into a bowl and scatter the mixed berries on top. Drizzle with the remaining 2 tbsp of olive oil and serve as a dip with the crunchy toasts.

PREP TIP
Toast the bread the previous day and store in an airtight container to keep them nice and crunchy.

banana bread

MAKES 1 (5 X 8-IN/
12 X 20-CM) LOAF

½ cup (80 g) almonds

1⅓ cups (300 g) butter

Generous pinch of salt

1¾ cups (300 g) coarse raw cane sugar,
    plus more for sprinkling

3 eggs

2½ cups (300 g) all-purpose flour

1 tsp baking powder

1 tsp ground cinnamon

3 very ripe bananas

Toast the almonds in a dry pan until golden, then chop roughly.

Preheat the oven to 340°F (170°C). Line a (5 x 8-in/12 x 20-cm) loaf tin with parchment paper.

Combine the butter, salt, and sugar in the bowl of an electric mixer; beat until you have a pale, fluffy, cappuccino-colored mixture.

Gradually beat the eggs into the butter and sugar mixture, working each one in well before adding the next. Then, stir in the toasted almonds, flour, baking powder, and cinnamon.

Peel the bananas, chop them into small pieces, and use a wooden spoon to gently fold them into the cake batter. Do not stir the mixture for too long.

Transfer the batter to the prepared loaf tin.

Sprinkle the top of the loaf with a bit of sugar, then bake for 60–70 minutes. Cover with a piece of aluminum foil as soon as the top looks like it is going too dark.

Remove the banana bread from the oven, leave to cool, then turn it out of the tin. Slice into pieces to serve.

PREP TIP
The banana bread can easily be made the previous day, allowed to cool, and stored in the fridge. Take it out of the fridge well ahead of time, remove from the tin, and cut into slices.

spiced zucchini and nut cake with cardamom and lemon frosting

Oil, for greasing the tin

7 tbsp (100 g) butter,
   at room temperature

1½ cups (250 g) raw cane sugar

1 tsp vanilla sugar

3 eggs

2 cups + 1 tbsp (250 g) all-purpose flour

3 tsp ground cinnamon

1 tsp ground allspice

1 tsp ground cardamom

2 tsp baking powder

1 tsp baking soda

½ tsp sea salt

12 oz (350 g) zucchini (courgette),
   coarsely grated

4½ oz (125 g) hazelnuts, roughly chopped,
   plus more for scattering

3½ oz (100 g) dark chocolate,
   roughly chopped

FROSTING

3½ tbsp (50 g) butter,
   at room temperature

1¼ cups (150 g) powdered (icing) sugar

1 tsp ground cardamom

Zest of 1 organic lemon

¾ cup (150 g) cream cheese

Preheat the oven to 345°F (175°C). Lightly grease a (8-in/20-cm) spring-form tin with oil and line the base with parchment paper.

To make the cake, in the bowl of an electric mixer, cream the butter and both sugars until light and fluffy. Add the eggs one at a time, mixing well after each.

In a separate bowl, combine the flour, cinnamon, allspice, cardamom, baking powder, baking soda, and salt, then sift these ingredients into the bowl with the butter, sugar, and egg mixture. Beat just until combined, then use a wooden spoon to gently fold in the chopped zucchini, hazelnuts, and chocolate. Mix well and transfer into the prepared cake tin.

Bake the cake for about 45 minutes. Test whether it is done using a wooden or metal skewer: The cake is ready if the skewer does not have any cake batter on it after being inserted into the center. Otherwise, bake the cake for a few more minutes, covering the top with aluminum foil if it is browning too much.

Remove the cake from the oven and allow to cool slightly on a wire rack. Then, remove from the tin and let cool completely.

For the frosting, combine the butter, powdered sugar, cardamom, and lemon zest in the bowl of your electric mixer and beat until well combined. Add the cream cheese and beat until smooth.

Cover the cooled cake with frosting, then sprinkle with some chopped hazelnuts if desired. This is an excellent sweet and spicy addition to your picnic spread.

PREP TIP

The cake can be baked the previous day and stored in the fridge. Thanks to the grated zucchini, it will stay beautifully moist. Prepare the frosting just before serving.

buckwheat waffles
with marinated strawberries
and tonka bean cream

SERVES 4

MARINATED STRAWBERRIES
10½ ounces (300 g) fresh strawberries
Zest and juice of 1 organic lemon
1 tbsp acacia honey
1 tbsp fennel seeds, finely crushed

TONKA BEAN CREAM
1 tonka bean
¾ cup (200 g) sour cream or
  crème fraiche
1 tsp acacia honey

WAFFLES
2 ripe bananas
4 tbsp butter, at room temperature
1 tbsp acacia honey
2 eggs
⅓ cup (50 g) buckwheat flour
¼ cup (30 g) almond flour
Pinch of sea salt

Carefully wash the strawberries in a bowl of cold water, then drain well. Hull and slice the strawberries into quarters.

In a medium bowl, combine the lemon zest and juice, acacia honey, and crushed fennel seeds. Toss the strawberries in this mixture, then set aside to marinate at room temperature.

Meanwhile, to make the tonka bean cream, grate the tonka bean into a bowl (5–10 times). Add the sour cream and acacia honey and stir well. Leave the flavors to infuse for 10–15 minutes at room temperature.

Peel the bananas for the waffle batter, and mash them in a bowl with a fork. Add half of the softened butter and the honey, mixing well. Whisk the eggs in a separate large bowl with a balloon whisk until frothy. Stir the banana and butter mixture into the eggs, followed by the buckwheat flour, almond flour, and salt, and mix until evenly combined.

Heat a waffle iron, and melt some of the remaining 2 tbsp of butter on the surface. Ladle some of the batter onto the waffle iron, and cook each waffle until crisp and golden yellow on both sides.

The waffles are best served lukewarm with the marinated strawberries and tonka bean cream.

PREP TIP
Marinate the strawberries in the morning. The tonka bean cream and waffle mix can also be prepared ahead of time and stored in the fridge. If you want, you can even cook the waffles in the morning and reheat them briefly in the oven until crisp.

caramel cream candy
with sea salt

1¼ cups (250 g) sugar

1¾ tbsp (25 g) butter

1 cup (250 mL) heavy whipping cream

1 tsp licorice powder

Pinch of sea salt

Vegetable oil, for greasing the dish

Powdered (icing) sugar or rice flour,
     for tossing (optional)

Slowly melt the sugar in a saucepan over medium heat, and allow it to caramelize. Be patient, and make sure the sugar does not burn or go too dark. Having said that, it is essential to cook the sugar enough to get a lovely, pale-brown color and an intense caramel flavor.

Carefully stir in the butter. Watch out! If it gets too hot, there is a risk of spitting.

Gradually pour in the cream in small portions, stirring constantly to make sure the caramel does not solidify. As the caramel slowly combines with the cream, you should get a pale-brown, viscous mixture. Cook for about 10 minutes.

Stir in the licorice powder and sea salt, and continue cooking until the bubbles in the caramel begin to connect and the mixture has developed a consistency a bit like porridge. If possible, check the temperature using a thermometer. A temperature of 260°F (125°C) gives you slightly softer toffees, while a temperature of 265°F (130°C) produces candies with a slightly harder consistency. The choice is yours!

Lightly grease a flat dish or baking sheet with a little vegetable oil, then spread the caramel mixture on top. Leave to cool until the mixture has reached a consistency that allows you to cut it into pieces that won't stick together. If the candies are still too sticky, you can toss them in powdered sugar or rice flour.

These caramel candies look particularly attractive packaged individually in paper candy wrappers. They also make a great gift for guests to take home.

PREP TIP
The candies can be made several days in advance. Store the wrapped candies in an airtight container at room temperature.

cherry nice cream popsicles with chocolate-buckwheat coating

MAKES 6–8 ICE POPS

Timing: Allow 3–4 hours for the popsicles to freeze.

3 ripe bananas

1 (14-oz/400-g) can coconut milk

10 fresh sweet cherries, pitted

3 tbsp peanut butter

Zest of 1 organic lemon

Sea salt

1 tbsp buckwheat

3 oz (80 g) dark chocolate

Peel and finely chop the bananas, then purée them in a food processor with the coconut milk, 8 of the cherries, the peanut butter, lemon zest, and a pinch of sea salt until you have a smooth consistency.

Divide the mixture among 6–8 small ice pop molds, insert a stick into each one, and freeze for 3–4 hours, until solid.

Toast the buckwheat in a dry pan until pale yellow.

Finely chop the remaining cherries.

Chop the chocolate, then melt it in a heat-resistant bowl over simmering water.

Dip each frozen ice pop briefly in the melted chocolate, making sure the ice cream itself does not melt. Immediately sprinkle with the chopped cherries and buckwheat, and serve as an ice-cold treat at the end of your fabulous birthday picnic.

PREP TIP
The ice pops can be made in advance and stored in the freezer.

birthday picnic
— menu planning
and preparation

Organizing a children's party can be quite a challenge, and that's before you start thinking about what food to offer! But if you plan carefully and keep the whole thing relatively simple, there will be lots of time for fun, games, and hygge—even for the party organizers.

THE PREVIOUS WEEK

RASPBERRY SODA WITH VERBENA (P. 204)
The raspberry syrup can easily be made a good couple of days in advance. The flavors will infuse beautifully while it is stored in the fridge. Add mineral water and ice cubes just before serving.

CARAMEL CREAM CANDY WITH SEA SALT (P. 228)
Make the caramel candy a couple of days in advance, pack in paper candy wrappers, and store in a cookie jar or airtight container.

CHERRY NICE CREAM POPSICLES WITH
A CHOCOLATE & BUCKWHEAT COATING (P. 230)
These ice cream pops can be made a few days in advance and kept in the freezer until ready to serve.

THE PREVIOUS DAY

CANDY-TOPPED BIRTHDAY BUNS (P. 208)
Make the yeast dough the previous evening. It can be shaped into balls and left to prove slowly overnight in the fridge. Bake the buns the following morning before the guests arrive.

WRAPS WITH EGG SALAD, PEAS, AND TARRAGON (P. 213)
Make the egg salad the previous day and keep in the fridge, so everything is good to go for assembling the wraps the following day.

RAW SUMMER VEGETABLES WITH
SUNFLOWER SEED DIP (P. 216)
Make the dip the previous day and store in a jar in the fridge (ideally covered with olive oil to prevent discoloration).

RYE TOASTS WITH RICOTTA AND BERRIES (P. 218)

Toast the bread the previous day and store in an airtight container to keep it nice and crisp.

BANANA BREAD (P. 223)

Bake the banana bread the previous day, allow to cool, and store in the fridge. Take it out of the fridge well ahead of time and cut into slices.

SPICED ZUCCHINI & NUT CAKE WITH CARDAMOM & LEMON FROSTING (P. 224)

Bake the cake the previous day and keep in the fridge. Thanks to the grated zucchini, it will stay beautifully moist and delicious. Prepare the frosting just before serving.

ON THE DAY ITSELF

RUSTIC PANINI WITH CHEESE, MORTADELLA, MUSTARD, AND BASIL (P. 212)

Assemble the panini a few hours before your guests are due. They can then be toasted just before you are ready to serve.

BUCKWHEAT WAFFLES WITH MARINATED STRAWBERRIES AND TONKA BEAN CREAM (P. 227)

The marinated strawberries, tonka bean cream, and waffle batter can be made ahead of time in the morning. The waffles definitely taste best when freshly cooked, but, if necessary, you can make these in the morning and reheat them briefly in the oven just before serving to make sure they are nice and crisp.

thank you

Anders, for another fantastic project—our fifth book together! I think we continue to improve and learn, and your wonderful photos always convey perfectly what is going on in my kitchen and in my world.

Sidsel, for all the lovely items you procured for this book. Thank you for always listening to me and Camilla, for understanding our ideas and making them a reality.

Julie Kiefer, for keeping everything under control and staying calm even when I came up with crazy ideas or did something else to rock the boat. Thank you for your unwavering belief in this project.

Sigrid Gry Laursen, for your expert supervision of all the different design elements, which you brought together with such attractive and harmonious results.

Hay, &tradition, The Table Project, Tekla, Akua Objects, Omnium, Norse projects, and Drakes, for providing gorgeous backdrops, bicycles, and fabulous clothes.

All our wonderful friends who posed for photos and ate with us.

My lovely family! Viggo, Konrad, Alma, Oscar, Ida, and Camilla: My favorite companions when it comes to hanging out and chatting over a delicious meal. Food plays a huge role in our family!

index

Library of Congress Control Number is available; a CIP catalogue
record for this book is available from the British Library.

Editorial direction: Julie Kiefer
Design and layout: Sigrid Gry Laursen
Prop stylist: Sidsel Rudolph
Illustrations: Anna Stahn
Translation from German: Alison Tunley
Copyediting: Peggy Paul Casella
Typesetting: Fotosatz Amann, Memmingen
Production management: Cilly Klotz
Separations: Ludwig Media, Zell am See
Printing and binding: Printer Trento Srl

Penguin Random House Verlagsgruppe FSC® N001967

Printed in Italy

ISBN 978-3-7913-8966-0

www.prestel.com